UNLEASHING the Power of Scripture

A Guide for Catholics

UNLEASHING the Power of Scripture

A Guide for Catholics

Mark Hart

Published by The Word Among Us Press
7115 Guilford Road, Suite 100
Frederick, Maryland 21704
wau.org

11 20 19 18 17 1 2 3 4 5

ISBN: 978-1-59325-297-7
eISBN: 978-1-59325-487-2

Cover design by Koechel Peterson & Associates

Made and printed in the United States of America

Library of Congress Control Number: 2017932032

Contents

Introduction

Growing up Catholic meant a lot of things to me. It meant serving Mass and getting to carry fire at the Easter Vigil. It meant crushing the toes of my unsuspecting brother with the kneeler when Mom and Dad weren't looking. Growing up Catholic meant feeling guilty for most sins (and some things that weren't actually sins), a love for plaid, prayer cards of bleeding saints, and a rosary on the rear-view mirror. Mass began at 10 a.m. sharp but ended at 11 a.m. dull, and only the promise of a chocolate donut from the Knights of Columbus table could keep this brat of God in line most Sabbaths.

Growing up Catholic also meant we had a Bible—a large, heavy, unopened Bible. There the word of God sat, on the shelf, untouched but impressive to random visitors. Had anyone taken the time to peruse that Bible, they'd have undoubtedly noticed, sadly, that each page was in pristine condition. Sure, the sacred writ may have made its way to the coffee table from said shelf on the annual evening that Fr. McGuire came over for dinner, but never did it make its way before our eyes. It didn't serve much purpose other than as a bookend, holding up all the other books *we actually did read*.

Sure, I'd heard the famous Bible stories growing up. Vacation Bible School gave me the basic gist of the kid-friendly classics—your David and Goliath, Noah's ark, Daniel and the lions' den, and at some point, Jesus' apparent healing of a leopard (imagine my surprise and relief years later when I realized it was a leper). These fanciful stories failed to inspire me, however, during my crucial preteen and high-school years. The Bible just didn't pique my interest enough to motivate me to read it myself or retain anything I heard from the pulpit.

As we grow, though, most Catholics who pay even moderate attention at Mass begin to notice a pattern. We hear of Abraham and Isaac and Jacob, even if we are unsure of how they were related or why that matters. We hear of angelic interventions, miraculous healings, and enough agricultural parables to choke a farmer. We watch as lectors struggle mightily to pronounce impossible names of forgotten places. We hear lineages and biblical names that would land modern parents and their children in psychotherapy. Can you imagine, for example, being named "Nimrod" (Genesis 10) or "Dorcas" (Acts 9)?

Sometimes we resolutely crack open Genesis in January with a New Year's plan to read the entire Bible, only to surrender in March—trapped somewhere in Leviticus with warnings against incest and rules regarding the treatment of wild oxen.

Still, there's something deep within most of us that finds the Bible special and enigmatic. Even if unread or misunderstood, the Bible means something. Even if our parents or grandparents didn't read it to us, many people do still read it. And even many of those who don't read it still think the Bible is important albeit confusing.

What Makes the Bible So Special: A Love Story

God reveals his love and providence to us in myriad ways. Consider a starry sky, a sunset over the ocean, or a baby's laughter. Assuredly, the Creator is seen throughout his gorgeous creation. But God's revelation is not limited to nature: just as freely as he reveals himself to us through created things, so does he reveal himself through his inspired word.

Written in more languages, read by more people, with more copies published and sold than any other written work in the history of the world, the holy Bible stands alone. Kings and rulers have outlawed it, wars have been waged over it, and millions of lives have been lost but also found because of it. God's divine revelation: inspired, entrusted, and gifted to us.

No other book will ever compare. Inspired (from the Latin *inspirare,* meaning "breathed") by God, recorded over a span of about seventeen hundred years by more than forty separate authors, and composed of seventy-three books of varying lengths and types—from songs to history, to letters, and more—the Bible is one of our greatest family heirlooms.

God's plan for our salvation, revealed in the Bible, is played out age after age, from the dawn of history. The danger for modern believers, however, is failing to see this history as just that: *his story*. Even more dangerous is the failure to understand that our stories are found in and wrapped up in God's.

Consider this: Jesus Christ could have chosen to teach us in a variety of ways. The fact that the Second Person of the Trinity chose to employ storytelling (parables) as his primary teaching tool tells us a great deal. Everyone loves a good story, and our story is part of the greatest story ever told.

As Pope Francis reminds us,

> So this love story began, a story that has gone on for so long, and is not yet ended. We, the women and men of the Church, we are in the middle of a love story: each of us is a link in this chain of love. And if we do not understand this, we have understood nothing of what the Church is.[1]

There's a reason that the Bible has been translated into every conceivable language (even Klingon for you *Star Trek* fans out there). There's a reason that, when Johannes Gutenberg—a Catholic—invented the printing press, his first print job was the holy Bible. There's a reason we still turn to one or two favorite verses to paint on a wall or tag an e-mail or scribble in a greeting card: after thousands of years, not even Hallmark can do better than "Love is patient. Love is kind." As beautiful as the works of Shakespeare, Austen, and Hemingway are, and as beloved their characters, their words are earthbound; they are not words inspired by the Holy Spirit about the Living Word who came down from heaven

The Bible is unlike any other book. The Bible is prayer, the very breath and life of God. It is the word *of* God, not mere words *about* God. That distinction necessitates our attention and demands reverence. That distinction should comfort you in your afflictions and afflict you when you get too comfortable. The journey to God is about joy, not happiness. Happiness is fleeting, but joy—the eternal joy of a life in Christ and life in heaven—that is eternal. We come to know that life in Christ quite literally through the Scriptures and in the sacraments. Only in knowing Christ will we come to know what it means to truly live.

As the Second Vatican Council affirmed,

> Therefore, since everything asserted by the inspired authors or sacred writers must be held to be asserted by the Holy Spirit, it follows that the books of Scripture must be acknowledged as teaching solidly, faithfully and without error that truth which God wanted put into sacred writings for the sake of salvation. (*Dei Verbum* 11)

As I have said—and at the risk of painful oversimplification—the Bible is not just *the* book but rather many books. The very word *Bible* comes from the Latin *biblia,* meaning "collection of books." And while this holy book is many books, it is, in reality, more of a letter—a love letter from the eternal Father to his children. It is the story of a bridegroom coming for his bride. It is a story less about hide-and-go-seek (though Adam and Eve start there) and more about being lost and found. It's the story of where we came from and where we are ultimately headed. Thus, knowing Scripture is truly a matter of life and death. Through the Bible, we learn not only how to avoid (eternal) death but also how to truly live.

The Purpose of This Book

Needless to say, this book will not answer all of your questions about Scripture. Nor will it offer deep exegeses about key passages. This is not an overview of covenant theology or a work of master apologetics. There are many books and courses that will help you take a deeper dive into the Bible. (I'll suggest some in a list at the end).

Instead, I offer this little book as an appetizer, an invitation and a purposeful inspiration for you to open your own Bible once again but with confidence and direction. I hope to unpack information that will allow this precious jewel to catch your eye and enrapture your heart once again or possibly for the very first time. I hope to give you entry points to pray with Scripture in new ways that will enrich your life—ways that you can share with your friends and loved ones so that they too will catch the fire of God's love found page after page. While the Mass is the source and summit of our faith—the pinnacle of our Catholic existence—Sacred Scripture (upon which the Mass is built) is available to you all day, every day, ensuring that when you're away from the parish, the Church is not away from you.

In this book, I will offer insights and suggest passages to read and places to start. I encourage you to open your Bible and read along (and aloud when possible) whenever you see a Bible passage in bold type. When you see a parenthetical reference, I hope you'll make the time to look it up, underline or highlight it in your own Bible, and come back to it and share it with others as the Holy Spirit leads. If you are uncomfortable marking up your Bible because it was a gift or an heirloom, that's okay, but I encourage you to get yourself a good study Bible you can write in. A worn-out Bible is the sign of a Catholic who isn't.

Consider these questions:

- Who are you in the eyes of God?
- Who are you created to be in God's sight?
- What is the unique vocation he has created you for?
- How will you know his will, and how do you listen?
- Are you willing to follow?
- What will your life look like if you do? If you don't?
- What do you do when you don't "hear" God?
- How does growing in knowledge of God through studying Scripture help you to better understand God?

The answers to these and countless other questions are waiting for you in the Good Book.

Always remember, Scripture is the true guide to a well-lived life. Once you start to read it, your life will never be the same—because you will discover that your life is no longer yours but his (**Galatians 2:20**).

CHAPTER 1

Old and New: When Past Meets Present

Imagine that two young men are walking down a deserted country road when they come upon a fence running across the road and obstructing their path. The first man says, "Look at this stupid fence blocking our way. This is pointless. I don't see any reason for this. C'mon, help me clear it away. Let's get rid of it so we can keep moving forward."

The second young man, however, has a different response: "The fact that we don't see the point in it is precisely the reason we shouldn't clear it out of the way! We need to stop and think about this. *Why* did someone, at some point, see the need to build this here? What is its purpose? If we can't figure out its intended purpose, beyond what we can see from our one minute of observation, then how can we just get rid of it? First, we think about it, then we discern if we should get rid of it."

Humility asks the questions that pride never thinks to ask.

This story, based on a famous analogy by G. K. Chesterton, illuminates one of the challenges of the Christian life: spiritual myopia. Chesterton lived in England during a time when Protestants and Catholics were at odds with one another and Catholicism was viewed negatively. "Out with the old" became something of a rallying cry for reformers who saw little of value in Catholicism's rich and prestigious history. But regardless of the context, Chesterton's story invites readers to ponder the value of the old versus the new and the distinctly different reactions of the young men.

The fence, for example, did not grow there on its own. Nor was it constructed by a pack of raving lunatics with no thought or purpose. At some point, someone must have created the fence out of a need. The fence served a purpose that the young men might not have quickly understood, though others before them did.

The point, in terms of spiritual myopia, is this: don't judge something negatively or destroy it just because you don't understand it. This insight is especially pertinent today, when the culture around us sees less and less of value in Christian faith and strives to ignore it or marginalize it or worse.

It is a terrible form of pride to think that everyone who came before us must have been foolish or less intelligent, that their faith contained little of use to them or holds any meaning for us today. Technology doesn't make us smarter than those who came before us. Consider what people accomplished *without* the help of computers or modern technology: they built pyramids without cranes, harvested crops without tractors, healed without prescriptions, and charted stars without high-powered telescopes.

The concept that old ideas are not as worthwhile or valuable as new ideas is both arrogant and dangerously shortsighted. Old ideas can be far better because they've held up over time.

The Big "Why"

Unfortunately, many people dismiss the Bible, the Catholic Church, or the holy Mass as antiquated and useless. These people have failed to pause, discern, and ask the big question, "Why did God give us these great gifts?"

I would submit that many of us fail to ask the question because of spiritual myopia. Amidst the hardships of life, it's easy to look down more than we look up. In times of disillusionment or confusion, we can often lose sight of God. In an increasingly atheistic culture too, it's more popular and commonly accepted to revere the telescope (the work of man) than to revere what you see through it (the work of God). What our ancestors called "the heavens" we refer to merely as "space." Modern minds have reduced God to a genie, Jesus to a hippie, and the Spirit to mere "energy."

But maybe the problem is this: before any of us can ask the "why" question, we need to take a step back and ask ourselves the "how" question—how to read these stories. The modern mind, for example, often struggles with the early chapters of Genesis. In just the first few verses, there are seemingly obvious contradictions. How exactly does God create light on the first day when the sun isn't created until the fourth? In a scientifically savvy, technologically advanced culture such as ours, the creation stories in Genesis 1 and 2 seem more like fairy tales or folklore than timeless accounts of ethereal truth.

Many questioning minds might be shocked to hear that the Catholic Church does not teach that we must interpret Genesis

1 and 2 literally. "God himself created the visible world," the *Catechism of the Catholic Church* says, and "Scripture presents the work of the Creator symbolically as a succession of six days of divine 'work,' concluded by the 'rest' of the seventh day" [Genesis 1:1—2:4]" (*CCC* 337). Catholics can believe that creation took six days or a far longer period, based upon how they see the evidence and provided that they are open to future insights, teachings, and judgments of the Church. The Church does remind us, however, that while the story is not scientific truth, it does teach us truths.

The author(s) of Genesis were not concerned with giving the reader a definitive, scientific explanation of how the world was created but were rather concerned with the "why." The *why* of creation, of life, of our distinction as men and women, of marriage, of sexuality and children, of life and death—that is the mystery we're being invited into in the world of early Genesis. Knowing this changes our mindset and speaks to the hopes of our hearts.

In the encyclical *Divino Afflante Spiritu,* Pope Pius XII explains very clearly the importance of guidance when we read the Scriptures, especially since very few of us have a strong command of the original languages and cultures from which they came:

> What is the literal sense of a passage is not always as obvious in the speeches and writings of the ancient authors of the East, as it is in the works of our own time. For what they wished to express is not to be determined by the rules of grammar and

> philology alone, nor solely by the context; the interpreter must, as it were, go back wholly in spirit to those remote centuries of the East and with the aid of history, archaeology, ethnology, and other sciences, accurately determine what modes of writing, so to speak, the authors of that ancient period would be likely to use, and in fact did use.
>
> For the ancient peoples of the East, in order to express their ideas, did not always employ those forms or kinds of speech which we use today; but rather those used by the men of their times and countries. What those exactly were the commentator cannot determine as it were in advance, but only after a careful examination of the ancient literature of the East."[2]

And so, the first question we must ask in Genesis should not be how the cosmos was created but rather, *why did God create it*? The answers to this and so many other questions about God and us and life and death all have the same answer: because God loves us. These answers are also found in the same place: Scripture. We must approach the holy Bible (and the holy Mass) like the second young man in the story, humbly seeking the answer after first asking the correct question.

There Is No "I" in *L-O-V-E*

And yet nowhere in Scripture does God utter the phrase, "I am love." No, St. John tells us (and quite emphatically in his first letter, I might add) that "God is love" (1 John 4:8), but we never hear Jesus utter the phrase, "I am love."

Why not? Jesus reveals himself to us in many ways and under many titles. Here are seven revelations of his divine identity from St. John's Gospel, for instance:

- "I am the bread of life." (John 6:35)
- "I am the light of the world." (John 8:12)
- "I am the door." (John 10:9)
- "I am the good shepherd." (John 10:11)
- "I am the resurrection and the life." (John 11:25)
- "I am the way, and the truth, and the life." (John 14:6)
- "I am the true vine." (John 15:1)

Seven different titles of self-revelation, but not one single "I am love" from the Lord. Christ never once uses the phrase, because love—true love—is *never* self-referential. Love is self-forgetful. Love always considers and desires the good of the other. "Love," as Pope St. John Paul the Great reminded us so often, is rooted in "the gift of self, without which the person cannot 'fully find himself.'"[3]

God is love (**1 John 4:16**). And God, since he is love, wanted to manifest that Trinitarian love and to offer that love to us in a tangible way (CCC 293–295). "God has no other reason for creating than his love and goodness" (293). Because love needs an object of love, God created the universe and all living things. But while all of creation is a reflection of the love of God, only men and women are gifted with free will. God formed a covenant with humanity (Adam and Eve) and gave us a sign of the covenant, the Sabbath. Man and woman chose self over God;

they sinned, and *literally* all hell broke loose. At that time, however, God also promised us a redeemer (**Genesis 3:15**).

Ever since "the Fall," God has been working to get us back to him. God's desire is to gather all of his children together with him in our heavenly home. To this end, God continues to give us every opportunity to live in right relationship with him, starting with a series of covenants revealed in Scripture. We are called to live in his love and to act in it; we are called to live as saints.

That pursuit of sainthood is (and always has been) beset on all sides by darkness, distraction, and obstacles. The Lord has drawn near to us, generation after generation, and we his bratty children have responded either in kind or in contempt, ever since we were "bitten" by the snake in Eden so long ago.

The Big Picture

Imagine that you're standing in a museum looking at a painting from several feet away. From this distance, you have a wide overview that allows you to see the broad "strokes" of the painting—how the whole picture flows together with its characters, colors, and shapes. This broad perspective is essential if you want to go more deeply into the specifics of the painting, such as the brush strokes.

In the remainder of this chapter, I'd like to take a similar step back to catch a broader view of the Bible, particularly those stories and promises of God known as covenants, which culminate in the cross and resurrection of Jesus Christ. Our point of view will not be that of our normal horizontal level but of a higher, almost "vertical" level. When the horizontal and vertical meet, we see the cross and the Father's much broader perspective.

Sacred Scripture includes hundreds of characters and was composed and compiled by many human hands, but always under the inspiration and guidance of the Holy Spirit. This masterpiece that is the Bible tells a consistent story about the one true God and his relationship with us, his people. The timeline of the story has a hinge point, a climax: the birth of Christ. This moment—so critical and incredible in human history—acts as a dividing point in the Bible, giving us what we commonly refer to as the Old Testament and the New Testament. Each is important for the story of our salvation: it would be a mistake to look at them as separate or as describing two versions of God or two different "gods" altogether.

And yet this division of the old and the new is commonly used as an argument against the validity of Sacred Scripture. Opponents of Christianity (and religious belief in general) are quick to point out passages in which God appears to be violent, oppressive, angry, or even the author of suffering. These images seem to contradict the loving, merciful God who is presented to us by Jesus in the New Testament. On the surface, this dissonance is unsettling. Did God suddenly change midway through Scripture? Is the God of the Israelite people different from the God of Christians and Jesus?

In fact, although there are passages in the Old Testament that disturb us, what we see primarily is the gradual unfolding of God's plan for humanity according to the times and the understanding of the peoples of those times. As Mark Giszczak writes in his book *Light on the Dark Passages of Scripture*,

> When we read the Old Testament, we have to be conscious of the gradualism of it all. The theology of Abraham is far more advanced than that of Adam, but the theology of Isaiah is far beyond even the theology of Moses. As time goes on and God reveals more and more of himself to his people, the picture fills out.[4]

God is the same yesterday, today, and forever, but our understanding of him is progressive, as is our relationship with him. Once we understand this—and books like *Light on the Dark Passages of Scripture* can help us do so—we will have the key to understanding the pattern of God's revelation and his great plan for us.

Even with that key, however, we are children before God and will never arrive at full understanding, no matter how hard we try. Maybe it would help to take a minute to think about the ways you understood the adults in your life when you were a child. Try to remember how you viewed your parents, teachers, coaches, and other important figures who helped you grow. Chances are good that you didn't understand everything they did or the rules that they made. It is possible that you thought your dad was a superhero or your mother the world's best and most loving mom. Perhaps, though, you struggled in your relationship with your parents and had opinions opposed to theirs.

Whatever your relationship was, as a child you probably saw your parents in very black-and-white terms, and you didn't always understand them. This makes sense—the rules, behaviors, and actions of your parents grew out of a life that you had no prior knowledge of or ability to relate to. If your mother told you to be home before a certain time, you may have felt it was unfair because you didn't understand the worry that a parent feels when a child is out late. Kids don't understand parenting because they just don't have the life experience of parents. But that doesn't stop children from trying to understand their moms and dads on their own terms.

This is true for us in everyday life, and in a similar way it was true for the authors of Scripture, whose understanding came out of their own limited experience and the shortcomings of their times. The Israelite people, for example, were often attacked by outsiders. Their lives were shaped by war and violence, and often this suffering came upon them when they became unfaithful to the Lord. At first glance, it may seem that God was being spiteful by punishing them or letting them suffer because of their sins—like a bad friend who gets upset and seeks vengeance. Rather, God was simply doing what a good parent does: setting limits, giving children the freedom to reject rules or make mistakes, and allowing consequences for wrongs committed.

The reality is that God is a God of love, and everything he proclaimed, enacted, and allowed in the Old Testament was a preparation for a time when things would become very new in the revelation of Jesus. "Many of the troubles [we see in the

Old Testament]," Mark Giszczak writes, "are rooted in the imperfection and incompleteness of divine revelation before Jesus. As the great divine teacher, God slowly but surely reveals more and more of himself throughout the Old Testament."[5]

Bound by Love

One way God reveals himself is through several key figures, their stories, and the promises that he makes. We call this type of promise that God makes with the people a "covenant." A covenant is more than a contract. A contract is an agreement to exchange services or goods. If you want your toilet fixed, you contract with a plumber. You agree to pay the plumber money, and he agrees to fix your toilet. He gets money, you keep your hands clean and your bathroom dry, and then you part ways.

A covenant, on the other hand, is something far more permanent and exchanges something far greater than services or goods. In a covenant, terms are set and promises are made, but what is exchanged is persons. The covenant is marked by a sign to remind the people of the promises that have been made and of their responsibility to fulfill their part of the covenant

Many people think of marriage as a contract, but it is actually a covenant and provides an easy way to understand what we mean by the term. In fact, matrimony is the analogy God uses most often throughout the Scriptures to communicate his intimate, eternal, and self-giving love. We, his people, are like a bride God marries and is bound to for eternity. In a sacramental marriage, a man and a woman make promises (or vows) to each other, exchange rings as a sign of their covenant, and give *themselves*—not money, materials, or services—to one another. A husband gives himself to his wife, and the wife gives herself to her husband. This is how God interacts with us as his people.

Six major covenants occur in Scripture and progressively reveal God's love for humanity. Each covenant helps us to grow in our understanding of his plan of salvation, culminating in the final and everlasting covenant in Jesus Christ. These covenants not only unfold God's plan of salvation; they forge unbreakable bonds between God and his people—and they are still essential for us today! They are at the heart of our understanding of Sacred Scripture and how we live our relationship with God day to day.

The Covenant with Adam and Eve

The narrative of Adam and Eve takes place almost immediately in the Bible. The first chapter of Genesis presents a poetic creation story. God creates order out of chaos, and creation culminates in the forming of a man and a woman in God's image and likeness. They are unique and the most complicated and intricate creations. God sets them apart for himself—he is going to have a special relationship with these two people.

This relationship is described in greater detail in the second chapter of Genesis, as God outlines the covenant that he will have with Adam and Eve. The word *covenant* is never specifically used but is absolutely implied. The terms of the covenant are spelled out in **Genesis 1:28—2:3**. God promises to bless the man and the woman. He charges Adam with the care of creation and establishes the seventh day (the Sabbath) as a day of rest and sign of the covenant.

Of course, this covenant is broken when Adam and Eve disobey God by eating from the Tree of the Knowledge of Good and Evil. This "original sin" breaks humanity's relationship with God, each other, and creation. But God is faithful to his covenant, even when we are not.

Read ***Genesis 1:28—2:3****, and then reflect on the ways that you uniquely reflect God and his specific call for you and your life.*

The Covenant with Noah

In Genesis 3, Adam and Eve commit the first sin by disobeying God's command and eating from the Tree of the Knowledge of Good and Evil. Genesis 4 gives us the next sin, murder. Cain murders his brother Abel and then lies about it to God. The result is exile, but sin has already begun to infest the world. The original disobedience of humanity toward God becomes a cancer, and by Genesis 6, God has had enough.

Humans become so wicked that God even feels bad that he made them; nevertheless, he is faithful to his covenant. God instructs Noah to build an ark to protect creation and save his family, because God is about to send a great flood to destroy "all flesh." While his neighbors think Noah is perhaps crazy for constructing a giant boat in the midst of good weather, Noah is following God's will—he is one of the last hopeful lights in a world darkened by sin. Fast forward: a great flood wipes out the wicked of the world, but a single family—Noah's—is saved.

Once the floodwaters recede, Noah gives thanks to God, and God establishes a covenant with Noah—this time God uses the word *covenant*—and promises that he will never again destroy the earth with a devastating flood (Genesis 6—9). Noah's faithfulness when the world around him was falling apart because of sin (and sin was certainly the norm) is met by God with the promise of fidelity that extends to all humanity. God tells Noah that a rainbow—the natural phenomenon that occurs when light shines through rain—will be a sign of this covenant, a persistent reminder that God is with humanity for the long haul, regardless of how bad things get.

Read ***Genesis 6:9–18****, and then reflect on the ways that God has carried you through a time of adversity or trial. Is there a sign that causes you to remember that time?*

The Covenant with Abraham

Even in the midst of idolatry, sin, and darkness, God finds and raises up people who are faithful. That is where God encounters Abram. In Genesis 12, we meet Abram, and the author tells us that Abram found favor with God. Abram's fidelity, however, undergoes tests and challenges. God promises to make Abram's descendants as numerous as the stars, and all seems right (Genesis 15:5). God gives Abram a new name—Abraham—and a son from his wife Sarah. That son, Isaac, is important. Without him, God's promise of descendants as numerous as the stars would become empty.

Imagine, then, Abraham's shock when God asks him to sacrifice Isaac (Genesis 22). This moment was more than a test of faith; it was a test of the covenant. Without Isaac, God's end of the covenant wouldn't hold up. It would be more than a contractual breach; it would be a severed relationship. But Abraham trusts that God's ways are above his ways and proceeds as directed. At the last moment, God intervenes and stops Abraham from sacrificing Isaac. Abraham's act of faith does more than justify him before God; it becomes a foreshadowing of how God will give his own Son as a sacrifice for us.

Read **Genesis 22:15–18,** *and then reflect on a time you needed to make a difficult decision in faith. How was God present to you in that time?*

The Covenant with Moses

Moses' story begins in controversy in Egypt, where the Israelites live in slavery. Though an Israelite by birth, Moses is taken in as a baby by the pharaoh's daughter and enjoys a life of privilege within the Egyptian royal courts. Years later, as an adult, he strikes down an Egyptian who is beating a Hebrew and, his life now in danger, quickly decides to go into exile. But God calls him back to lead his people out of slavery. Moses becomes the greatest prophet in Israelite history. He is not simply a spokesperson for God; he speaks with him in a relationship that is closer than any other person enjoys with God. They speak "face to face" (**Exodus 33:11**).

Moses leads the people out of slavery in Egypt and mediates a covenant with God that is inaugurated with the Passover. The Israelites become the chosen people and are brought into the covenant by keeping the Passover feast, which is to be practiced and remembered forever. It is a condition of the covenant.

Moses is the greatest leader in Israelite history. In many ways, he is a foreshadowing of Christ: God promises to raise up another prophet like Moses (**Deuteronomy 18:15**) who ultimately is Jesus, the one who inaugurates the new covenant at Passover.

Read ***Exodus 3:2–12****, and then reflect on a time when you stood on "holy ground." What was it like? How did you know it was holy ground? How did God speak to you in that moment?*

The Covenant with David

King David, one of the greatest kings in the history of Israel, was born in Bethlehem of humble means, was the youngest and smallest in his family, and was working as a shepherd when God chose him to be Israel's leader. He became the mediator of a new covenant that would establish the Israelite people as a kingdom. David's life was not always filled with holiness—he was at times mired deeply in sin. At one point, he committed adultery, then had the husband of the woman he violated sent to the front lines of battle to be killed.

God punishes David but also blesses him, and he makes a covenant with David that his throne will endure forever. It is from the household of David, via St. Joseph, that Jesus is born; hence the oft-used title in Scripture, "Son of David."

Read ***Psalm 51****, a psalm traditionally attributed to David after his sin of adultery. When have you been in need of God's mercy? Where are you in need of mercy now?*

The Eternal Covenant with Jesus

The final covenant is with Jesus, the Son of God, and it is the fulfillment of all the covenants made prior to him. Through his cross, death, and resurrection, Jesus ushers in the new covenant, which he begins on the night of Passover at the Last Supper. This new covenant that Jesus ushers in will not be written on stone but on the hearts of the people (**Jeremiah 31:31–34**).

Jesus invites all people into this covenant and asks that we follow him as disciples, participate in the Eucharist, and believe what he taught. This covenant is the most critical of the six. It is the last covenant that God makes with humanity until the end of time.

Read ***John 19:28–30****, and then reflect on the magnitude of Christ's sacrifice for you. Consider this "exchange of self" that a covenant offers in light of the holy Eucharist. Have you ever taken a few moments to thank him for this sacrifice? Take some time now to do that.*

In all of these covenants and throughout salvation history, we are not simply encountering episodes or stories; we see *our* story. We see ourselves in the ups and downs, and we see a God who refuses to give up on us and goes to great lengths to find us, redeem us, and bring us home. We see not only that this story is our story but also that God will continually invite us into a deeper relationship with him.

CHAPTER 2

His Story Is Our Story: Finding Yourself in Scripture

The Bible contains the stories of many famous "major" characters such as Moses and David, whom we met in the last chapter, as well as others, such as Jacob, Elijah, Mary, and Paul. There are plenty of "minor" characters as well, like Rahab, Gideon, Hosea, and Philemon. Some are key players in the history of salvation, and others play smaller roles, but all are pieces of the great puzzle.

Scripture features sin-filled failures, heroic lives, and miraculous encounters. These are not designed to *wow* you into loving God but should remind you that the Bible is filled with characters, both saintly and unsaintly, who were embroiled in the same battle against sin as you and I are, every day.

But don't make the mistake of thinking that "character" means fictional. You *too* are a character in God's story of salvation (**1 Peter 1:8–9**). You are not an unnamed person in the story of creation. You are not an "extra." You are the protagonist. God knows your name (**Isaiah 43:1**). God created you (**Psalm 139:13–16; Jeremiah 1:4–8**) and knows everything about you (**Matthew 10:30; Isaiah 55:8–9**).

Getting Started

The word of God will challenge you, inspire you, and give you hope. The word of God will bring you joy. The word of God might confuse you too. For this reason, every time you open your Bible, you should pray and ask the Holy Spirit, the author of Scripture, to open your mind and your heart to receive what God has for you. We must avail ourselves too of the knowledge of the Church and the Magisterium—the teaching authority of our pope and bishops—holding up our thoughts to the sanctified x-ray of truth to see if they match up and, if not, why not. The Magisterium, led by the Holy Spirit, guides our scriptural interpretation and keeps us on sure footing, even as the culture around us changes from age to age.

Keep in mind too that, although the Bible is not fiction, it is a collection of different types of writing serving different purposes. Taking those forms into account is crucial. Is a particular book prophetic? liturgical? historical? apocalyptic? What was the intention of the sacred writer in composing the book? As Vatican Council II affirmed,

> Attention must be paid to literary forms, for the fact is that truth is differently presented and expressed in the various types of historical writing, in prophetical and poetical texts, and in other forms of literary expression. Hence the interpreter must look for that meaning which the sacred writer intended to express and did in fact express through the medium of a contemporary literary form. (*Dei Verbum* 12)

All the books of the Bible, whatever their form, communicate the truth and articulate God's love for his people—for you. In fact, you can find a little of yourself in virtually every person in Scripture, male and female alike. As the great Danish philosopher and theologian Søren Kierkegaard said, "When you read God's Word, you must constantly be saying to yourself, it is talking to me and about me." The Bible, of course, isn't just about getting to know ourselves. Even more, it offers us insight into the mind and the heart of God. It's through the word of God that we come to understand more fully how God thinks and what he wants for us and from us.

Entering the Story

As you try to discern what God has for you—what role you play in this incredible story—it might help to consider the various ways that you can get to know people: you can hear about them from other people, you can check out their social media profiles, or you can watch firsthand how they interact with others. If they're famous, you might even catch interviews with them or read books about their lives. None of these methods, however, are nearly as effective as sitting with a person, one on one, and asking meaningful questions, like

- How does it make you feel when . . . ?
- Where did you grow up, and what was your childhood like?
- What are you most afraid of?

- When do you feel the most joy?
- Why do you do what you do?
- Who is your personal hero?
- What roles do God and faith play in your life?

Questions like these skip past the shallow things we usually talk about, helping us to really get to know a person. They reveal a person's true identity.

While you can use these questions to get to know other people, they are also great starting points for getting to know yourself. Where does your identity come from? Where do your beliefs come from? What do you base your decisions on? These and similar questions should lead you back to one fundamental truth: God is the author of your life.

As author, God has breathed you into existence as a character in his story. God created you; he loves you and wants you here. God has a plan for your life (see **Jeremiah 29:11** and **Ephesians 2:10**), and if you really want to "know yourself," as so many desire but so few actually do, the best and fastest way to do that is to get to know the One who created you.

And the Bible is one of the greatest ways to get to know the author of *your* story, because by reading about his interactions *with other characters,* you can get to know how God thinks and moves. By observing and studying how others have responded to him in the past—in right and wrong ways—you will gain both insight into how to live in the present and wisdom that will help you move confidently toward the future. Customs and traditions might change, but when you read

Scripture, you'll see that people don't change all that much. You have more in common with biblical characters than you might have thought! Knowing what did and did not please God in other people is a great way of knowing what does and does not please God in us.

In this next section, I'll introduce you to several characters and to moments within their individual stories. Some you might know well. Others you might not recognize at all. Some are heroic, some are heartbreaking, but they're all thoroughly human and have something to offer that will help you grow in your faith. Learn from them. Learn too that living as a Christian is not so much about finding yourself as it is about finding and unleashing Christ's presence and power within you. The more you recognize God's presence in you, your home, your school, the Church, and the world, the better you'll be able to share God's love with all you meet

Exercise One: Really, God? Really?

There are many famous stories from Genesis, but few draw the collective wince from readers as the sacrifice of Isaac does. We took a look at the story in the last chapter, but now let's dive even deeper. It's been asked over the centuries, "Why would a good and loving God ask Abraham to sacrifice his very own son, Isaac? Is God just bloodthirsty?"

In reality, human sacrifice was quite common in the world during the time of Abraham (roughly 2000 BC). We read in the Bible of groups like the Ammonites and the worshippers of Baal sacrificing their children to their gods. What was odd about God's request of Abraham, however, is that it was inconsistent with what Abraham had come to expect from God and the promises God had made to him.

As you prepare to read this story again, approach it as though for the first time. Pay attention to each detail. How long was the journey to the mountain? What was the name of the mount? What was the son carrying, and what was the angel's response?

We have the benefit of hindsight when reading and hearing the story, but imagine yourself as Abraham or Isaac and as if the action was unfolding in real time before you.

Open your Bible, and read Genesis 22:1–14.

Now, put yourself in Abraham's sandals. Why did God tell Abraham at the outset of the journey what was going to transpire? Why didn't God wait the three days, until father and son were approaching their destination, to tell Abraham what this journey would entail? Withholding that information would have undoubtedly made the trek far more enjoyable and bearable for Abraham, would it not? What does this say to us about the mind of God? Is he a God of the bait-and-switch—allowing Abraham to think he and Isaac were on a carefree father-son trip and then switching it up at the last minute? If not, then what does this teach us about God's interest in working with his people, with us, in a forthright manner? What do we learn about total abandonment to his plan?

Did God leave the site up to Abraham, or did he ask him to follow a carefully orchestrated plan? What did Isaac carry up the mountain, and why is it significant that the "only son" carried it? What had to be built before the sacrifice could be offered? After the angelic intervention, what did Abraham end up sacrificing, and what was it caught in?

When we pause to really pay attention to the details of this famous story, the Holy Spirit can connect the dots in new ways. The better we know the story, the more easily we can see the natural parallels between the sacrifice of Isaac and the sacrifice of Christ. Interestingly, as a good Catholic study Bible might point out in the footnotes, there is a geographical connection that places Moriah and Calvary within the same immediate area. Moriah is not solely one mountain or mount; rather, the word actually identifies a range of small mountains or hills outside of Jerusalem.

Two thousand years after Abraham built an altar and prepared to sacrifice his only son to God, our Lord Jesus Christ carried the wood for his sacrifice up one of Moriah's hills, known by its Latin name, *Calvary*. These two distinct events transpired in the exact same region. The same ground that was soaked with Abraham and Isaac's tears of joy and pain and that produced the thicket that trapped the ram (a male lamb) would one day, years later, yield similar thorns for our Savior's crown and also be soaked with the blood and sweat of our Savior, Jesus, and the tears of our Mother Mary.

Journaling Prompt: Consider the forethought and omnipotence of God as demonstrated in this story, and remember it the next time he asks you to take a path you're reluctant to walk or to undertake a task you are afraid will end poorly. Journal about a time you trusted God and it went well, one in which God demonstrated again his fidelity.

Exercise Two: Up on the Roof

Sometimes we forget (or try to forget) that God sees all. Everything. One of the Bible's most famous stories of sin and its effects happened when King David forgot—or ignored!—this fact. It was "late one afternoon" when David got off his couch (2 Samuel 11:2). He was alone. Though his armies were off fighting, the warrior-king remained back at the palace. He strolled out onto his massive rooftop, and from there he saw a beautiful woman bathing. At this moment, David had a choice.

Open your Bible, and read 2 Samuel 11:1—12:13.

David stood there, a powerful man confronted with a simple decision. He could look away to protect the dignity of the woman and his own chastity, or he could let his eyes go where they need not. The choice lay before him, where two paths diverged in the spiritual wood: holiness or sin. He was standing at the crossroads of temptation. Rather than looking away, David chose himself, allowing his own lust to get the better of him.

Using his royal position, he sent for the woman, Bathsheba, who was the wife of Uriah the Hittite, one of David's warriors. As if adultery were not a heinous enough crime, he then hatched the plot to have Uriah killed in battle.

How did this happen? How did David go from being the anointed one, the one with whom God was so pleased, to the one who was so selfish, so lustful, and even murderous?

Have you ever done something you knew you weren't supposed to do? Have you ever looked at someone in a way that stripped away his or her dignity? Have you ever done something you're ashamed of in an effort to cover up something else you've done? An obvious parallel here is to the temptation of pornography, which begins with lust and with an interior battle of self(ishness). It begins with the desire to look where you shouldn't look.

Long before the Internet or cable television, lust was still very much a struggle. Maybe you know the temptation of looking where you shouldn't, at things that you shouldn't. Maybe you know too the guilt and shame that bind the soul, that are a natural byproduct of using others. That's what sin does: it replaces freedom with slavery, life with death.

You're not alone.

We all sin. We all fall short of God's hopes and expectations for us. We may be tempted at different times and in different ways, but we are all tempted to sin in some way. We have that in common. You're not the only one who is tempted. You're not the only one who sins. Your parents were tempted. Your grandparents were tempted. The pope is tempted. Your parish priest is tempted. Adam and Eve were tempted (and you know how that turned out). Even Jesus was tempted, but Jesus didn't sin.

God knew you'd be tempted. He also knows that you can resist all temptations with his help. Check out what it says in 1 Corinthians 10:13:

> No temptation has overtaken you that is not common to man. God is faithful, and he will not let you be tempted beyond your strength, but with the temptation will also provide the way of escape, that you may be able to endure it.

To repent means to turn away from sin (darkness) and turn back to God (light).

Did you notice what Scripture says there? *It doesn't say you won't be tempted; it says you won't be overcome by it.* No temptation is beyond your strength, because God always provides a way out if you call on him. He promises you that you can withstand and endure even the hardest temptations. Not because of how strong you are but because of how strong he is.

Yes, David sinned. David also repented. He was sincerely sorry, so *he went to the Lord to make it right.* If you've sinned, trust in God's mercy. There is no sin too big for God to forgive. No sin. The only sin God won't forgive is the sin you don't ask forgiveness for. God doesn't force his mercy on anyone, but he's dying to give you his mercy. That's what the crucifix is: living proof that God is dying for you to know how much he loves you.

Journaling Prompt: What are the times of day, places, relationships, or moods that most often lead you to sin? What can you do to change your patterns of behavior or communication or circumstances to more proactively and aggressively fight against sin in your life? What (if any) are the reasons you don't go to the Sacrament of Confession more often? And what are you willing to do to avail yourself of God's mercy more frequently?

Exercise Three: The Eye of the Beholder

Esther was born at a difficult time in Israel's history. A long line of kings (both good and bad) had come to an end, Jerusalem had been destroyed, and most of the Jewish people had been deported to Babylon. Soon after, Babylon was taken over by Persia. The Jewish people were thousands of miles from their home and at the mercy of a foreign ruler.

A Jewish orphan growing up in Persia, Esther was raised by her distant cousin, Mordecai. She was exceptionally beautiful (Esther 2:7), which was both a blessing and a curse. When Vashti, the Persian queen, publicly embarrassed her husband, King Ahasuerus, the king began looking for a new bride. Esther was among the young women chosen as a possible queen, and she was taken to the palace, along with others, for preparation and training. From this pool of women, the king would choose the next queen of Persia. It was the Bible's own version of a beauty pageant.

Esther caught King Ahasuerus' eye and eventually became his new queen. Though married to him, law and custom forbade Queen Esther from approaching the king or entering his court unless he summoned her. Any other attempt to approach him was punishable by death.

After Esther became queen, the king raised a man named Haman to a high rank in the court and ordered everyone to kneel and bow to him at the royal gate. Mordecai refused, on religious grounds, and Haman became enraged against Mordecai in particular and all the Jews in general. He hatched a plan to destroy them, manipulating King Ahasuerus into ordering a decree for the slaughter of the Jews.

When Mordecai learned of the Jewish people's fate, he secretly contacted Queen Esther, asking her to approach the king and to save their people.

Open your Bible, and read Esther 4:1–17.

Queen Esther was now faced with a dilemma: If she approached King Ahasuerus without being summoned, she could be charged with contempt in the king's court, publicly embarrassing him (as had the former queen), and very likely she would be sentenced to death. If she did nothing, her beloved cousin and guardian, Mordecai, would be put to death and the Jewish people would be destroyed.

So Queen Esther prayed. She asked the Jews in the city, Mordecai included, to join her in prayer and fasting for her impending visit to the king. All of them put on ashes and sackcloth, symbols of mourning and repentance. (That symbolism, in part, is why we have ashes on Ash Wednesday.)

On the third day of fasting, Queen Esther rose from the ashes and sackcloth, prepared herself, and entered the court of King Ahasuerus. Each step she took was proof not only of her trust in God but also of her courage and selflessness. In the rest of the chapters in the Book of Esther, you can (and should) read of Queen Esther's brilliant plot to both save her people and ensure that Haman would not harm anyone ever again. Mordecai had raised Queen Esther to worship the one true God and not the false gods of the Persians. When it mattered most, it was Esther's intense love for her God and for her people that allowed her to save the day by doing what no one thought possible.

We live in a world that is obsessed with outward beauty and physical power. But Esther knew that true beauty and true power come from God's Spirit within. Her outer beauty might have turned heads, but in the end, it was her inner beauty, her love for God and for her people, that saved souls.

God put Esther in the right place at the right time, but she had to tap into the Spirit of God within her if others were to be saved. She had the power, but she had to pray to unleash it.

God has you right where he wants you too. You have the power too. God gave you the Holy Spirit, "a Spirit of power" (**2 Timothy 1:7**), when you were baptized and confirmed. Through the sacraments, God's life, his grace, fills you. The Holy Spirit, dwelling within you, makes you beautifully dangerous and wonderfully powerful (**Philippians 4:13**). Unleash that power with a loving heart, and you too will be known for your virtue and heroism.

Journaling Prompt: Are you courageous enough to follow God's will even if it leads to personal peril? Have you ever been afraid to speak up, fearing what might happen to you if you do? What are some situations, even small ones, in which God is calling you to be more heroic or more vocal about your faith?

Do you love others enough to put yourself on the line? Why or why not? Do you seek personal comfort and avoid conflict over sharing God's truth? Read **Matthew 7:1** and **Luke 17:3**, and write a few lines about how they are similar but, more important, how they are different.

Now for exercises four and five. Rather than giving lengthy context for each story, I'll just give you reading prompts along with some thoughts for reflection and journaling. See if you can identify with these next two characters.

Exercise Four: Short, Smart, and Saved

Read Luke 19:1–10.

What made Zacchaeus climb the tree that day? Sure, he was short, but that's still a lot to go through just to see someone. Yes, Jesus was developing a quasi-rock-star celebrity status—but tree climbing? It was so impulsive and so uncivilized. Others in the town had heard of Jesus. Many turned out—although doubtless some did not, thinking that Jesus wasn't worth the time. So why was Zacchaeus different? Why did grace move in his heart on this particular day, to get him to drop what he was doing and put himself in a position where the Lord could speak to him?

But lack of dignity aside, all Zacchaeus really did was climb a tree for Jesus. That's all it took. He put forth the effort to see God, and God noticed—and responded in kind. Zacchaeus climbed a tree to catch a glimpse of mercy. Mercy would be nailed to a tree to offer Zacchaeus a glimpse of heaven and the love-filled sacrifice required to get there. His story invites us to ask ourselves what we need to do to catch that same life-changing glimpse.

Journaling Prompt: Can you relate to Zacchaeus at all? Answer the following questions, and record your answers in a journal for further reflection.

- Have you ever had "everything" and realized that, in reality, you had nothing?
- Would *you* risk embarrassment or your reputation or even your job for the sake of Jesus?
- Are you willing to do anything different in order to "see" Jesus more clearly?
- Is the crowd around you the reason you can't see Jesus clearly?
- Are you afraid to break out of your routine or your comfort zone?
- When Christ looks at you and calls your name, do you respond or look away?
- When the Spirit convicts your heart, do you admit your wrongdoing or redirect blame?
- Are you seeking only personal forgiveness, or do you desire to make restitution to those you have hurt along the way?

For Zacchaeus, salvation came knocking that day. How many days has salvation come knocking, come seeking *you?* He stands at the door of your heart, knocking (see **Revelation 3:20**). Picking up the word of God, you scale the sycamore. The question is whether or not you want the adventure to continue. Once you turn this page or finish this book, do you have the courage to come down and to live in even greater abandonment to Christ?[6]

Exercise Five: The Road of Life

Read Acts 9:1–9.

So there Saul sat, blinded and humbled. Everything he knew up until that trip to Damascus had changed, but it wasn't just Saul's world that was changing. God was doing something greater, something internal, something far less obvious and far more profound: God was changing Saul from the inside out. God was recreating Saul; he was making Saul new. The God Saul encountered that day was different from the God he had come to know on his own. When Saul was humbled, he was startled; when he was blinded, he began to truly see. That's what grace does: it gives us the eyes of faith.

Journaling Prompt: Can you relate to Saul at all? (We know him, by the way, under his Roman name—Paul. Having two names was quite common in his world at the time.) Answer the following questions, and record your answers for further reflection.

- When you think of your sins, do you consider that they not only grieve and hurt other people but grieve Jesus himself? Think of an example.
- How would you describe your experience or vision of God? How does Paul's intimate and personal experience of God challenge you to consider your own relationship with God?
- Do you feel as if God *knows* your name and even calls you by name?
- Have you been feeling as if God doesn't notice you or seem to care about what you do? If so, why?
- Is your vision of God one of an absent Father who is far from active in your life, or is it one of a loving, ever-present Father?

If some of these questions strike a nerve in you (as they do in me), then perhaps your vision of God needs to change—just as Paul's did.

Paul's calling and ultimate success (for the kingdom) should give all of us great hope. No matter how sinful we have been, no matter how prideful we could ever be, God is willing to use us if we are willing to change. God has a plan for you that he crafted before your conception (see **Psalm 139:14–16**), a plan that only you can fulfill (see **Jeremiah 1:5–10**). Often we cannot clearly see or hear God's plans for us because we are so consumed by our own.

Have you encountered God in a personal way? Do you know and relate to Jesus Christ in an intimate way? Which

Paul do you connect with more—the one prior to conversion or post-conversion? Is it about what God does "through you" or what God does for you and in you? Do you go to Mass out of obedience or out of love?

If you haven't had that encounter in your life yet, that *aha* moment when you just *know* that God is real, that Christ is present, and that you're a sinner and in need of God's mercy, it's time to think again. What are you doing to give the Holy Spirit a shot at your heart? Are you falling on your knees and crying out to God to save you from your sinfulness, your brokenness, and ultimately yourself? Take a page out of Paul's book—which is to say, out of the Bible—and invite the Lord to reveal where you may be blind, that you might truly see clearly.

The Rest of the Story

At this point, you may notice a bit of a pattern within the covenants mentioned in chapter one and these stories of faith laid out in chapter two. God, in his love, finds ways to shake us out of our own best-laid plans (see Hebrews 12:26–29). The gentleness or force with which he shakes us normally corresponds to the degree of our stubbornness and sin. Too many of us, when God calls, run the other way. But as Paul learned, you can't outrun God. Once shaken, we are broken, and only then can we be remade more perfectly into Christ's image. The formula goes something like this: shake, break, remake.

Which of the three stages are you currently in, and what are you allowing God to do? If you're not willing to let God change you—to radically transform you—who is really the God of your life? The Light of the World doesn't come forth from a genie's lamp. No, the Lord is the Good Shepherd coming for his lost sheep. Often the lost are actually grazing in the pews on Sunday, and that is the perfect place to shake, break, and remake disciples with the word of the Lord.

CHAPTER 3

Contrary to Popular Belief: Dispelling Common Catholic Misconceptions

God is the (ultimate) author of the Bible (see *CCC* 105).

Some people have a difficult time with that statement. It's safer and more convenient to say that people were writing *about* God rather than acknowledge the truth: the Bible is the living word *of* God (**Hebrews 4:12**). But the writers of Scripture aren't giving their "take" on God; rather, God is breathing words through the pens of men. Did God utilize the different talents and gifts for writing, communication, and storytelling of each author? Absolutely. He used their gifts the same way he still uses people's gifts in ministry every day.

The Bible was inspired in a unique way, at a unique time in God's plan of salvation and in history. No other book is now or ever will be a *living* word; no other book can bring you, in a such a life-changing way, into the very heart of God. This divinely inspired gift is not meant for the select few but for the masses. God's intention was not for his word to be hidden but for it to be shared. Many Catholics are surprised to hear that the Church encourages us to encounter God in Sacred Scripture daily, but that's not the only surprise when it comes to Catholics and the Bible.

Challenging Your Knowledge

I've always liked the phrase "contrary to popular belief." It gets your attention. It challenges your knowledge.

For instance, contrary to popular belief, Cleopatra was not Egyptian, bats are not blind, Moses climbed Mount Sinai not once but many times, and camels do not carry water in their humps.

Right now, you may be thinking, "Okay, great, Mark. Thanks for the useless knowledge and for wasting the last ten seconds of my life." But here's my point: these "facts" reveal a disturbing trend, namely that mistruths presented often enough as facts have a way of making themselves quasi-factual in our thinking. It requires conscious effort to name mistruths and correct them in an intentional way, lest these misconceptions keep us from truth. The pursuit of truth is the pursuit of God, who is "the way, and the truth, and the life" (**John 14:6**).

So what does that mean for us as we pursue the study of Scripture? It means that some of the things we think are true about Catholics and Scripture are not true. As I've traveled the globe in ministry for the past twenty-plus years, I've noticed a pattern among Catholics in regard to particular mistruths.

- Contrary to popular belief, Catholics actually do know the Bible (at least far better than they think they do).
- Contrary to popular belief, the Catholic Mass and the early Church predate the Bible as we know it today.
- Contrary to popular belief, everything in the Bible can speak to us today.

- Contrary to popular belief, the Catholic Church did not add books to the Bible.
- Contrary to popular belief, you can understand the Bible and study it on your own (with a little help and direction).

There are plenty of other misconceptions about the Bible and the Catholic Church, but I'd like to tackle these five points to get us all on the same page (pun intended) before we dive more deeply into his word.

Contrary to popular belief, Catholics actually do know the Bible. Cradle Catholics are often quick to tell me, sometimes in a sheepish tone, "You know, Mark, I'm embarrassed that I know so little about the Bible. I mean, *I went to Catholic school!*"

So did I, and while I'm grateful for the education and also for the self-discipline I acquired, one thing my parochial schooling failed to do was instill in me the desire or tools to really dig deep into God's word. Let's be fair here. We have a lot to learn as Catholics. I mean, on top of Sacred Scripture, we've got a lot to keep straight: holy days, sacraments, and saints to help us overcome every ailment from bad driving to bowel disorders. We are supposed to remember when to avoid meat, which mysteries of the Rosary fall on which days, and the correct responses to Mass prayers even when those around us don't know the responses (like at a wedding . . . what pressure!).

The truth is that most of us lack the confidence to just open the Bible and begin reading. But if we've been going to Mass year in and year out, we have been immersed every Sunday—and every day of the week if we're daily Mass-goers—in Scripture. And not just because of the readings from the Bible that take place during every Mass. From beginning to end, the Mass itself is steeped in the Bible. We aren't aware of how much biblical knowledge we actually have, even if we aren't exactly sure of the chapter, verse, or book that a passage came from.

Just for fun (we'll take a more in-depth look at the Mass later, in chapter six), let's see how well you know your Bible based simply on spoken prayers and responses from the Mass. See if you can finish these phrases in your head:

- "In the name of the Father, and of the Son, and ______________."
- "The Lord be ___________."
- "Glory to God in the highest, and on earth ________________."
- "Lift up your hearts. We _______________________."
- "May the Lord accept the sacrifice at your hands __________________."
- "Lord, I am not worthy that you should enter _________________."
- "We proclaim your Death, O Lord, and _________________."
- "The mystery of _____________."
- "You never cease to gather a people to yourself ______________________."

- "The grace of the Lord Jesus Christ, and the love of God, and the _______________ be with you all."

Any Mass-going Catholic recognizes most, if not all, of these phrases. They are so engrained in our subconscious that we can finish the phrase without even thinking. Did you know that every one of these phrases comes directly from Sacred Scripture? Below are (some of) the citations for these specific prayers and responses.

- In the name of the Father, and of the Son, and of the Holy Spirit. (see Matthew 28:19)
- The Lord be with you. (see Ruth 2:4)
- Glory to God in the highest, and peace on earth to people of good will. (see Luke 2:14)
- Lift up your hearts. We lift them up to the Lord. (see Lamentations 3:41)
- May the Lord accept the sacrifice at your hands for the praise and glory of his name. (see Psalm 50:23)
- Lord, I am not worthy that you should enter under my roof. (see Matthew 8:8)
- We proclaim your Death, O Lord, and profess your Resurrection until you come again. (see 1 Corinthians 15:3–5; Revelation 22:12)
- The mystery of faith. (see 1 Timothy 3:16)
- You never cease to gather a people to yourself, so that from the rising of the sun to its setting, a pure sacrifice may be offered to your name. (see Psalm 103:17; 113:3)

- The grace of our Lord Jesus Christ, and the love of God, and the communion of the Holy Spirit be with you all. (see 2 Corinthians 13:14)

Okay, I think you get my point. Even outside of the Mass, however, you've encountered Scripture—and probably even quoted from it—without necessarily knowing it. Have you ever uttered or heard these popular phrases?

- The blind leading the blind. (Matthew 15:14)
- Turn the other cheek. (Matthew 5:39)
- By the skin of your teeth. (Job 19:20)
- Holier than thou. (Isaiah 65:5)
- A leopard can't change his spots. (Jeremiah 13:23)
- Keep the faith. (2 Timothy 4:7)
- Good Samaritan. (Luke 10:30–37)
- Eat, drink, and be merry. (Ecclesiastes 8:15)
- A wolf in sheep's clothing. (Matthew 7:15)
- The writing on the wall. (Daniel 5:5)
- The apple of one's eye. (Deuteronomy 32:10)
- A drop in the bucket. (Isaiah 40:15)
- An eye for an eye. (Exodus 21:24)

While there is always more to learn and—more to the point—*retain* when it comes to the word of God, from your participation in the Mass alone you have a stronger base than you might realize. Before we can go any further, , it's important to know where the Bible came from and why. That can help us to get to where we are going.

Contrary to popular belief, the Catholic Mass and the early Church predate the Bible as we know it today. A close examination of the Gospels reveals that Jesus himself never wrote a thing—unless you count his scribbling in the dirt before an angry mob (see **John 8:1–11**). He didn't come to write a best seller. Surprisingly enough, he didn't even tell his followers to write anything down.

Instead, he chose to gather people together to teach them about the kingdom of God and to form them into a community founded on Peter and the apostles. He formed a community that we now call the Church. This Church began when the Holy Spirit came down upon the apostles, and they began to preach the gospel and invite people to follow Christ and be baptized. It was not until later that the writings of the New Testament (and eventually the Bible as a whole) were produced by this Church.

The Church did not come out of the Bible; the Bible *literally* came out of the Church.

Have you ever thought about this? Most of us who have grown up in a Christian tradition have probably never considered a time without the Bible. We know that Jesus did not come with a Bible in hand to give to his followers. He did have the Old Testament (which, by the way, wouldn't have been called the "Old" Testament in Jesus' time; it was simply referred to as Scripture), but even the earliest parts of the New

Testament were not written *until at least twenty-five to thirty years after Jesus' death and resurrection*. Further, as we've seen, the New Testament wasn't written down in one sitting by one person. The New Testament is a collection of different writings, written by different people at different times and places, and addressed to different audiences.

You may have heard the word *canon* used in regard to Scripture. *Canon* comes from a Greek term meaning "measuring rod" and is the term used to describe which biblical books "measured up" and were included in what we now call the Bible. The Old Testament was already written when Jesus arrived on the scene, but in the decades following his ascension, dozens of "gospels" and hundreds of other writings began to make their way around, each with its own unique spin on the life of Christ—some accurate, most inauthentic. And so the process of sorting out the works to include in the New Testament canon began to take shape. There are a few important things to note about this.

First, the life of Jesus and the works of his early followers were almost entirely shared through speech, not writing, in the years immediately following Jesus' death. In other words, they were handed on as oral tradition. Second, there was only one Church during the time the New Testament writers were at work. In the beginning, if you were Christian, you were Catholic, as it was the universal Church founded by Jesus. (*Catholic* comes from the Greek term *katolikos*, meaning "universal.") These early Christians believed in such truths as the Real Presence of Christ in the Eucharist, as we see reflected in several books of the Bible.

Lastly, it was this Church that finally put the Scriptures together in the form Catholics know today. It took years to formalize the full canon. Travel was difficult, illiteracy common, communication slow, and transcription costly. Christianity was a deadly venture too, as the Church endured persecution while at the same time exploding in growth.

It took many years of prayer, conversation, discernment, and debate by bishops, scholars, and leaders to determine, under the guidance of the Holy Spirit, which books were truly inspired. Finally, at the Councils of Rome (AD 382), Hippo (AD 393), and Carthage (AD 397), the list of accepted books was set. It's the same list you hold in your hands when you hold a Catholic Bible today. The Council of Trent (1545–1563) formally defined this canon for us, partially in response to the decision of the Protestant reformers to remove seven books from the Old Testament. But the canon as Catholics know it is the same as that affirmed by the Church since the fourth century.

So why does any of this matter? Because *contrary to popular belief*, the Bible was not the standard used by the early Church to judge what was true to Jesus' message It couldn't have been; it wasn't around yet. Rather, *apostolic teaching* was the standard. This teaching was found in the Church, specifically in the teaching of the popes and bishops appointed by Peter and the apostles to continue the mission entrusted to them. This is why St. Paul tells St. Timothy that the Church is "the pillar and bulwark of the truth" (see **1 Timothy 3:15**).

It is the Church that guarantees the truth of the Bible. As St. Augustine said, "I would not believe in the Gospels were it not for the authority of the Catholic Church."[7] It is only because the Church is guided by the Holy Spirit and has a share in the authority of Jesus Christ that we even have the Bible in the first place.

Contrary to popular belief, everything in the Bible can speak to us today. I love Sacred Scripture for many reasons, one of them being that there are so many random, seemingly unimportant details found in its pages. They fascinate me. While they might seem unnecessary, however, they are not. Remember, the Bible was inspired by the Holy Spirit, and *everything* can be useful if we pray about it long enough.

I've spent a lot of time over the past several years sharing Bible stories with people of all ages. No matter if the audience members are teens, children, or adults, some stories always grab everyone's attention and are ripe for reading and sharing: Balaam's talking donkey (see **Numbers 22**), for example, or Elisha and the she-bears (see **2 Kings 2**), or Eutychus' fateful nap during St. Paul's homily (see **Acts 20**), to name a few. I don't spend a majority of time on them, but they do pique people's interest and leave them wanting more. These stories begin great conversations. They elicit good questions. They ensure that a Bible study can be fun and not just formational.

Below are a few random verses, details, facts, and tidbits that, in a spirit of fun, illustrate how seemingly nonsensical facts can prompt deeper reflection and aid us in our faith walk.

Did you know that

1. Abraham had two nephews named Uz and Buz (Genesis 22:21)?
2. Hezekiah is not a book in the Bible?
3. God said that the people in Nineveh didn't know their right from their left (Jonah 4:11)?
4. a live dog is better than a dead lion (Ecclesiastes 9:4)?
5. the Lord whistles (Isaiah 5:26; 7:18)?
6. Paul was bitten by a snake while building a fire, then mistaken for a god (Acts 28:1–6)?
7. Job's three friends were named Eliphaz, Bildad, and Zophar (Job 2:11)?
8. Job's wife thought he had bad breath (Job 19:17, *New American Bible*)?
9. Ahasuerus had people read the chronicles of his reign to him to help him sleep (Esther 6:1)?
10. the Levites had a mandatory retirement age of fifty (Numbers 8:25)?

On the surface, none of these facts contains soul-shaking insight. The more I prayed about them, however, the more I found the randomness quite useful to me personally. Just so, fun (or not-so-fun) facts like these can lead you on a path of reflection that helps you move forward in your faith journey.

For example, here's where you could end up if you stopped to pray and reflect on those ten passages.

1. Abraham had two nephews named Uz and Buz (**Genesis 22:21**). Did you also know that Timothy's mom was named Eunice and his grandmother, Lois (**2 Timothy 1:5**)? You might not know Abraham or Timothy's family tree, but do you know the names of your neighbors, your co-workers, and the people who worship next to you at Mass each Sunday? We pray the "our" Father, not the *my* Father. We are a family of believers. It's time we got to know our brothers and sisters better.

2. Hezekiah is not a book in the Bible. Hezekiah was, however, a king who reigned twenty-nine years in the southern kingdom of Judah. Almost three decades of service, and most people know nothing about him. What is your goal in life? To serve or to be recognized?

3. God said that the people in Nineveh didn't know their right from their left (see **Jonah 4:11**). Whether or not this annoyed God, think about how annoyed *you* become with people who don't "get it." Look closely at your life. Do people who don't act or think like you steal your joy? Don't lose heart or hope. Jonah was surprised by Nineveh's humility and penitence when he delivered the message calling them back to God. People might surprise you too. Give them a chance.

4. A live dog is better than a dead lion (see **Ecclesiastes 9:4**). In short, where there's life there's hope. It might seem trite, but it's true. You can always come back from defeat or whatever weighs you down if you reach out to the Lord and to

others for help. Hope—it's one of the three theological virtues. If you're not feeling it, pray for it, and ask others to help you find it.

5. The Lord whistles (see **Isaiah 5:26; 7:18**). Yes, it actually says that. You should whistle too. It's hard to whistle when you're stressed and hard to stay stressed when you whistle.

6. Paul was bitten by a snake when building a fire after being shipwrecked off the coast of Malta. The natives were amazed that he didn't swell up, keel over, and die. They decided he was a god (see **Acts 28:1–6**). The Lord is most likely doing amazing things through you, but you're not a god. Keep your head about you. Stay humble.

7. Job's three friends were named Eliphaz, Bildad, and Zophar (see **Job 2:11**). Do you know who your kids' and grandkids' friends are? Where do those friends stand with God? Have you ever talked with them about your own faith life?

8. Job's wife thought he had bad breath (see **Job 19:17**). Another translation just says she found him repulsive. Not good, either way! Fresh breath is an evangelization must. Halitosis is not part of holiness. This is part of loving thy neighbor: brush frequently, and use mints as needed.

9. Ahasuerus had people read his chronicle of notable deeds to him to help him sleep (see **Esther 6:1**). If you can't sleep,

ask your spouse or a friend to read Leviticus to you. It's not the most thrilling reading, but it's still useful!

10. The Levites had a mandatory retirement age of fifty (see **Numbers 8:25**). Wouldn't that be nice? What was their secret, you might ask? The Levites were the priestly tribe, so they had a nice benefits package. That being said, they also had a strong rhythm of prayer. You may not be able to retire at fifty, but with a solid prayer life, you could look forty when you retire at sixty-six!

Obviously, some of the above "insights" are offered tongue-in-cheek. And that's my point: studying Scripture can be fun as well as informative and transformative. The word of God is serious business, but we need not treat it like a grind. As G.K. Chesterton reminded us, "Angels can fly because they can take themselves lightly."[8] God laughs (see **Genesis 21:6; Psalm 2:4**), and you should too. It's not about having random knowledge; it's about realizing that anything can point creation back to the Creator. God is love (see **1 John 4:8**). Live in that love. Share that love.

Contrary to popular belief, the Catholic Church did not add books to the Bible. You might sometimes hear people say that the Catholic Church *added* books to the Bible. That's not the case!

It is true that the Catholic Bible has seventy-three books and the Protestant Bible has sixty-six, but how did that circumstance develop? Both have twenty-seven books in the New Testament, but they disagree about the books in the Old Testament. There are two different canons of the Old Testament from ancient times: the Palestinian Canon (which is used in the Protestant Old Testament) and the Alexandrian Canon (which is used in the Catholic Old Testament). Why the differences? What books are missing from the Protestant Bible? Read on.

The missing books in question are Tobit, Judith, Wisdom, Ecclesiasticus, Baruch, 1 and 2 Maccabees, and parts of Esther and Daniel. The Hebrew Bible (the Old Testament) was written in Hebrew (imagine that!), but as the Greek language became more dominant, seventy Jewish scholars translated the Hebrew Bible into Greek. This happened between 250 and 125 BC, and the translation is known as the Septuagint—which is Latin for "seventy."

By the time Christ was born, Greek was the common language of the Mediterranean world, and so the Septuagint was very popular. Jesus and all of the New Testament writers would have been familiar with the Septuagint. In fact, the Septuagint was the version of the Old Testament that the New Testament writers used as a reference when they wrote their individual books. (Any time they quoted the Old Testament, they quoted from the Septuagint.)

This canon of the Old Testament was accepted as *the* canon for fifteen hundred years, until the Protestant Reformation. In 1529, Martin Luther, the leader of the Protestant Reformation, decided to use the Palestinian Canon, consisting of thirty-nine books, as his Old Testament canon. He chose this canon, which had been developed for various reasons by rabbis shortly after the time of Christ, because it related to Luther's understanding of doctrine and Tradition. For example, the Palestinian canon does not include Maccabees, which refers to praying for the dead.

So if your Bible's Old Testament contains the forty-six books of the Septuagint, then you are using the same Old Testament canon that Jesus, the apostles, and the New Testament writers used and that the Catholic Church has used for the past two thousand years.

Contrary to popular belief, you *can* understand the Bible and study it on your own. Reading and studying the Sacred Scriptures is the journey of a lifetime. Now, as with any journey, there are several different routes you can take to get to where you want to go. Some routes are faster but more difficult. Some routes take a little longer but offer a smoother ride.

Many people set out to read Scripture with the fastest route in mind; their goal is to finish and "conquer" the Bible as quickly and easily as possible. That route is treacherous.

I want to encourage you to take your time on this journey. I also want to point out a few potential potholes and obstacles that might slow you down or make you want to turn around or quit altogether.

Five Things to Be Aware of When Reading the Bible

1. Don't get lost in translation.
There are hundreds of different translations of Scripture available today, far too many to list here. Basically, Scripture is translated in two principal ways:

- The formal equivalence method: The person (or group) translating tries his or her hardest to match the original text word for word or phrase for phrase *as closely as possible*, while still making the new translation readable.

- The dynamic equivalence method: The person (or group) translating is not as concerned about matching *words* as he is about matching *thoughts*. Basically, it's a meaning-for-meaning translation rather than a word-for-word translation.

Depending on which method the translators used, you could be reading a translation of a translation of a translation. So obviously, the particular word you are reading could have a different connotation than when it was first expressed. Footnotes and commentaries are helpful in sorting out the original meaning(s), what the original words were trying to convey.

2. Don't assume that other cultures thought the way you think.
Our twenty-first century is so different from ancient Mediterranean culture and from the times of ancient Palestine that it

can be difficult to fully understand some of the customs and cultural references in the Bible. You might read sentences or sections that leave you feeling confused, disgusted, or even angry. Before you get too worked up, however, imagine how past generations would think of your life.

Imagine how easy someone from biblical times would consider your life to be, given that you have cars, air conditioning, microwaves, and cell phones, for example. But those technological and cultural advancements don't necessarily mean your life is easy, just different. In the same way, the simplicity of ancient biblical times doesn't mean that people were stupid or their behavior was gross, just that they lived with different challenges and obstacles. Take the time to learn about their culture before you dismiss or judge it as antiquated.

There are literally hundreds of resources you can consult, from books to websites, that will tell you about Jewish culture, geography, customs, and so forth. Take the time to read this information; it's really interesting stuff.

3. Don't get overwhelmed by the geography or pronunciations. When it comes to biblical geography, you're probably no expert. Facts about ancient cities in the Middle East, for example, are probably not part of your everyday conversation. As a result, you might get frustrated or even demoralized when reading Scripture because, not only are you unable to find most cities and sites on a map, but you can't even figure out how to pronounce some of them.

Don't get overwhelmed. Remember, times and places change, but the truths are timeless. Nevertheless, the stories contained within the pages of Sacred Scripture happened in actual places, not fictional locations. And so getting to know even a few facts about the geography or the culture can make a huge difference in your understanding of a situation or in the lesson you draw from it.

The word "*Bethlehem*," for instance, means "house of bread." That fact might not have meant a lot to the people in the time of King David, who was born there, but it sure carries a deep meaning to us who realize that the Bread of Life, Jesus, was born there. As you study Scripture, it's not as essential to know geography as it is to know certain other facts, but the more effort you make to locate cities and learn a few facts about them, the more the stories will come to life in your life.

4. Don't think that random details are useless.

There will be moments when you will read a story or passage and say to yourself, "Why is *that* in there? Why was *that detail*, something so random, included in the Bible?" The temptation is to say, "That's useless to me in the twenty-first century," and just move on. The challenge, however, is to look deeper and ask yourself why that fact was inspired, recorded, and preserved for future readers.

For example, you might be reading about the storm at sea in Mark 4 and come to the line that says, "[Jesus] was asleep in the stern on a cushion" (**Mark 4:38**). You might ask yourself, "Why do I need to know where Jesus was sitting in the boat or the fact that he was on a cushion and not on wood? What difference does that make to the story about how he calmed the storm?"

The better response? Look for deeper reasons why the author included such details. In this case, the stern and the cushion can point to an eyewitness testimony: only an eyewitness would have seen them or communicated them. Maybe that means that Mark was in the boat with Jesus or that someone who was in the boat (like Peter, who traveled with Mark later in life) communicated the intimate details of the story to the author. Get the idea?

Don't ever think that random details are just random. They were important at one point, and if we look deep enough, they're probably still important on some level.

5. Don't dismiss names or family trees as unimportant.
Have you ever been at Mass or been reading the Bible on your own and come across a family tree (lineage)? You know, it's one of those phrases that says, "So-and-so begat so-and-so, and then so-and-so begat so-and-so." The normal response when one of those lists begins is to jump ahead to "the stuff that matters."

Those lists do matter, however, even if they don't mean a lot at first glance. Knowing which people were connected to one another—and the circumstances and sin and virtue that shaped certain family trees—helps us get a better grasp not only of biblical characters but also of how similar our families and lives are to those of our ancestors in the faith. Knowing where we come from is essential for knowing where we are headed. On a very practical level today, for example, knowing there is a history of alcoholism or cancer in a family tree allows us to be more proactive about our own health

Look at **Matthew 1:1–16** for a few moments. How many of the names on that list do you recognize? They might not seem that important, but Matthew knew they were. Not only did his Jewish audience need to know the genealogy (the ancestral bloodline) of Jesus Christ, but they also needed to see some of the non-Jewish people in Christ's family tree. Those verses that begin Matthew's Gospel appear unimportant, but even a quick study of the five women listed there reveals much about the family, life, and mission of Jesus Christ.

Keep these things in mind as you navigate the Scriptures, and write down the questions you have as you go along. Study solid Scripture resources, attend parish or diocesan Bible studies, and talk with people at your parish who are knowledgeable about the Bible—priests and deacons and religious sisters and catechists, for example—and you will find answers to many of your questions.

CHAPTER 4

You *Can* Do This: An Introduction to *Lectio Divina* and the Liturgy of the Hours

"If only I could hear God's voice speak to me, it would be much easier to have faith." Thousands, if not millions, of people throughout the history of Christianity have spoken that line. If you've been taking this book seriously and have begun a journey into Sacred Scripture, perhaps this thought has crossed your mind as well.

God has spoken directly to prophets in the past, the disciples were privileged to know and follow Jesus when he walked the earth, and throughout the Acts of the Apostles, we see the early Church performing mighty deeds and receiving visions. Wouldn't it be easier to be a Catholic if we could have the same experiences or talk to God every once in a while? Like, even just once?

Jesus Christ is the same yesterday, today, and forever. He is still speaking to us through the Holy Spirit, but perhaps we have forgotten how to listen. Our prayers become litanies of "help" requests or half-hearted recitations of Hail Marys. But prayer is both active (speaking) and passive (listening), and although God sometimes comes to us in big moments and revelations, more often he is found in the quiet spaces and moments of our day. We can hear him if we just take time to listen.

A prophet named Elijah finds God in silence while he is hiding on a mountain. He is running from Jezebel, an evil ruler who wants him dead because he serves the true God, the God of Israel. God promises Elijah that he will meet him on the mountain but instructs Elijah to wait in a cave until the right moment.

Take a minute to grab your Bible and read the passage for yourself—**1 Kings 19:9-13.**

God doesn't announce his presence with any of the traditional methods—lightning, thunder, earthquake, wind—but in a "small voice." Some translations read that God was revealed in a "tiny whispering sound" or "the sound of sheer silence." Elijah would've missed that cue if he wasn't listening and paying attention to all of the other events taking place.

Lectio Divina

God wants to speak to you and guide you today, according to his own plans, and if you are still holding that Bible, then you have your meeting ground. He didn't give us Sacred Scripture simply to study, dissect, or pursue in a scholarly fashion. Certainly, we can do all of those things, and they will help us grow in our faith. But there is another kind of reading that we can do with Sacred Scripture, a divine kind of reading, that isn't as focused on backgrounds or contexts and is more concerned with how the Holy Spirit is using the word of the Lord to impact our heart.

We call this kind of prayer *lectio divina.* It is a rhythm of prayer that uses Sacred Scripture as a means to listen for that "small voice" of the Holy Spirit. Lectio divina is an ancient practice in the Church, and although St. Benedict helped develop it and made it an important part of the Benedictine religious tradition, countless lay people, priests, and religious outside of that order have made it an essential part of their prayer lives. The prayer itself is simple; all you need is a Bible, some quiet space, and some time.

Before I explain the prayer, it is important to identify what lectio divina is not. First, when we pray through Scripture using lectio divina, we are not doing a Scripture study. As I've said before, it's good to know the background of what we are reading, what some of the theological terms mean, and who the characters are. Those things can strengthen our prayer. But in lectio divina, we aren't going to take time to look at footnotes or pull out a biblical concordance to look up the history of a location or etymology of a particular word. These are important and necessary parts of learning the Bible; they just aren't things we do when we are praying in this manner.

Second, lectio divina is not about getting some earth-shattering revelation. Don't enter into it thinking that walls are going to shake and God is going to answer all your questions and fix your problems and speak to you directly from the pages of Scripture. When we enter lectio divina (and really, any prayer) with an agenda, it rarely turns out well. Go into the prayer open to receive whatever God wants to give you. It will be exactly what you need.

Finally, lectio divina is not hard to learn, but it does take practice. It involves periods of active prayer and passive prayer.

We are comfortable with the active part of the prayer but may be less comfortable with the passive part. We are accustomed to *doing* things in prayer, not simply being. Don't get discouraged if you feel as if the prayer isn't going well or if you are having a hard time "getting it." Prayer involves practice, and the more you pray, the better you will become at it.

How to Pray Lectio Divina

There are four movements to lectio divina, and each has a Latin name that will make you sound very theologically adept around friends. The four movements are *lectio*, *meditatio*, *oratio*, and *contemplatio*. You have probably already guessed that these words in English mean "reading," "meditation," "prayer," and "contemplation." Each movement alternates between active and passive.

Lectio

This active movement of prayer begins with choosing a Scripture passage to read. The length and content of the passage are important; this isn't a time to play Bible roulette and just flip open Scripture and start reading. The Holy Spirit can absolutely speak through any part of Sacred Scripture, but it will be easier to hear him in this type of prayer when we are reading through the beatitudes rather than through Levitical law or the instructions for making an ark.

Length is also important. Reading an entire chapter from a book of the Bible is great for study but not for this kind of prayer. Choose a short narrative by looking at subheadings (if your Bible has them), or just choose a few verses to read through. At the end of this chapter, I've listed seven short passages with solid content that you can use to get started as you explore lectio divina. Mass readings for the day are another great place to find a passage to use.

Once you've chosen a passage, it's time to start prayer. Begin by making the Sign of the Cross and asking the Holy Spirit to be with you and to guide your prayer. Then begin reading—it can help to read out loud. You are going to read through your passage three times, slowly. This isn't speed reading. You are allowing the words to roll over you. As you read, be aware of a word or phrase that stands out for you. It may seem to resonate or jump off the page. Hold on to that word; you'll need it for the next part of the prayer. It is likely that this particular word, phrase, or even image is something that God wants to use to speak to you.

Meditatio

After reading through your passage three times (slowly), enter into meditation with that word or phrase that stood out to you. This is a passive prayer. Don't be concerned with figuring out insights or with dissecting the word or phrase. Use it as a mantra, and simply repeat and meditate on it over and over again.

The early Benedictine writers described this process quite pleasantly. They encouraged practitioners to ruminate on the word, as a cow chews cud. For those not agriculturally inclined, you should know that cows digest their food partially in their mouths. This involves chewing, swallowing, throwing the food back up into their mouth, chewing some more, and repeating the process. It takes a while and breaks the food down into something that can be easily digested.

And this is how we are encouraged to meditate. I told you it was pleasant. . . .

We want to simply let those words be our focus. Other thoughts, images, words, or distractions may enter into our prayer. That's all right; the worst thing you can do is try to ignore them. Instead, acknowledge the distraction but don't follow it, and then return to your meditation. There is no time limit for the *meditatio* phase. As you practice lectio divina, you will start to have a sense for when you need to move on. For now, set a timer for five minutes for your meditation time. Then work to increase it by one minute each day until you hit ten minutes.

Oratio

For those who prefer to do something while you pray and are still nauseous after that cud reference, you will be happy that we are returning to active prayer with *oratio*. Most of us will be comfortable with this part of lectio divina. We take time to ask questions of God, to seek answers from God, to make prayers of petition to God. We dive more deeply into what we meditated on.

Perhaps your meditation spurs something inside you that causes you to enter into a deeper dialogue with God. This is a great place to bust out your journal and start writing. At the top of the page, be sure to put the Scripture passage that you are reflecting on and the word or phrase that stood out to you. Later on, this journal can be a powerful witness to the ways that God has moved (and is moving) in your life.

Contemplatio

From active back to passive. This is one of the most challenging parts of the prayer. After the reading, the meditation, and the prayer, we contemplate. This movement is simply pondering the goodness of God and sitting in gratitude for the grace that God has poured into your life. It is living Psalm 46:10, "Be still, and know that I am God." Simply be. Allow thoughts to come and go, but be mindful that you are in God's presence and that he has poured grace out to you in the Scriptures. It is just that simple (and also that difficult). Ultimately, contemplation is about sitting with all that was given through the word of God and allowing it to sink in.

Getting Started: A Few Practical Pointers

The best way to get started praying lectio divina is to find a quiet space where you won't be disturbed, grab your Bible, and put your phone into airplane mode. It can help to light a candle to draw your focus and to remember that the light of Christ dispels darkness (see John 1:5) and will illuminate your heart through the word. Before opening your Bible, spend a few moments in serious and silent prayer. Focus on your breathing, in and out. Ask the Holy Spirit to enlighten your mind and open your heart.

As you turn to the Bible and read a passage, envision the scene. Watch for adjectives. Pay attention to details. Really "enter into" the moment. If you're in a Gospel, lock eyes with Jesus. See the lion beneath the lamb's exterior. Allow the Gospel to inspire and challenge you, to shock and comfort you. Listen closely with the ears of your heart as your heavenly parent calls *you* by name. And be thankful that, by virtue of your baptism, you are God's child and your name is written in heaven (Luke 10:20).

Dedicate around twenty minutes to praying with the passage you have chosen. Set a timer if you need help keeping track of the time. Each movement gets about five minutes, no more and no less. Be mindful of where you struggle or feel tempted to cut corners. Give those areas extra attention and effort.

Here are a few suggested readings that can jumpstart and provide rich imagery for prayer:

- **1 Kings 19:9–13:** This is the story I used at the opening of this chapter. There is a lot to pray through here, especially if you are thinking about how God's voice is present in your life.

- **Psalm 139:1–13:** This psalm focuses on how God knows us perfectly. Great to pray through if you are feeling distant from God.

- **Matthew 14:25–33:** Jesus walks on water, and Peter wants to try it out as well. The dialogue in this narrative is great for any time you feel afraid to step out and be bold in your faith.

- **John 1:1–5:** The opening of the Gospel of John is considered "high Christology," but that shouldn't scare you away from praying through the forceful words that reflect on the power and presence of the word of God, Jesus Christ.

- **Romans 12:9–18:** St. Paul provides a list of what an ideal disciple looks like. By itself it is convicting, but through prayer, it becomes even more challenging, as the Holy Spirit identifies specific areas we need to work through.

- **Philippians 2:5–11:** This is one of the earliest Christian hymns. It is a beautiful poem about Christ's humanity, divinity, and humility. Great around Easter (or anytime).

- **1 John 3:1–3:** St. John's letters are quick reads, but this short passage packs a punch as it quickly identifies who we are and to whom we belong.

These few passages should get you started, but there are many more that offer entry into prayer. Look for them, remember them, and start that journal. Once the word begins to transform your life, you will find yourself coming back to lectio divina again and again, and your life will never be the same.

Let's move on to another ancient tradition of prayer, one that can unite you to brothers and sisters throughout the world, as they, like you, lift their minds and hearts to God each day.

The Liturgy of the Hours

Breathe in and breathe out. You'll take thousands of breaths like that today yet hardly realize it. Breathing is automatic, a barely noticeable rhythm that's tied directly to your survival. As you pull air into your lungs, your heart beats and pumps through your veins with life-giving oxygen—and you're probably not going to give it a thought unless something suddenly goes wrong.

Life is made up of such essential biological rhythms. Our circadian rhythm controls when we fall asleep and when we wake up. Our metabolic rhythm determines periods of hunger and signals when to eat. These forces hum along in the background, allowing us to function efficiently, to develop habits and routines while expending little additional mental energy.

We know how devastating it can be when these rhythms are disrupted. If you spend all night tossing and turning, worried about a big meeting or test the next day, you are going to feel the effects the next morning. Now, turn that sleepless night into a week of them, and suddenly returning to a normal routine is much harder. Routines and rhythms—whether essential to life or healthy additions to life—keep us moving along.

The Church too, in her wisdom, provides us with a rhythm—in this case, of prayer—that helps sustain us. Lectio divina provides one type of rhythm; the liturgical seasons and the intentional cycle of readings at Mass provide another. The liturgical cycle calls us to recognize the natural progression of life and death and points us toward life eternal. It celebrates even the ordinary moments of life with two seasons of Ordinary Time, recognizing that our extraordinary God is present in situations and circumstances that seem routine or mundane—even "boring." The liturgical seasons provide a flow and context for the Mass, offering unique readings for each season and calling us to reflect more deeply on Christ's kingship, life, death, and resurrection.

In short, the Church recognizes the natural flow and rhythm of seasons and invites us to see the handiwork of God within that. The Church also recognizes that, as our lives change, as our world alternates through times of war and peace, and as our personal lives and communities move somewhere between order and chaos, we need a rhythm of prayer that keeps us grounded in what is eternal.

To this end, the Church offers another rhythm of prayer that is the same throughout the worldwide Church and is deeply rooted in Scripture—the Liturgy of the Hours. The Liturgy of the Hours is a collection of prayers separated into offices or "hours" that span the day. There are seven: Lauds (morning prayer), Terce (midmorning prayer), Sext (midday prayer), None (midafternoon prayer), Vespers (evening prayer), and Compline (night prayer). The final "hour" is called the Office of Readings.

The prayers, as you can see, are designed to be spread throughout the day rather than prayed all at once. This rhythm is intentional. Not only does it keep the person praying the Liturgy of the Hours grounded in prayer, but it also ensures that someone is always praying on behalf of the Church. (Anyone can pray this way, but priests, deacons, and religious brothers and sisters make promises to pray the offices every day.) Since the hours are spaced out and time zones vary, at any given moment, including right now, people are praying the Liturgy of the Hours on behalf of the Church. They are keeping the rhythm alive and petitioning for our needs and our world.

Where to Find the Liturgy of the Hours

The Liturgy of the Hours has, for centuries, been compiled in a book or series of books known as the breviary. Historically, this is the book priests, religious, and others have used to pray these prayers. There are two print editions of the breviary that Catholics are familiar with. *Christian Prayer* is a single, substantial volume that contains all of the necessary Scripture and prayers, grouped under general headings in separate sections of the volume in order to save space. Different colored ribbons help readers mark the various sections so that they can flip back and forth to the prayers and readings at the appropriate time. This requires a learning curve, but once a person masters the navigation, *Christian Prayer* is simple to use.

There is also a four-volume set that contains greater detail and is somewhat easier to navigate but is much more expensive. Most people opt for the single-volume version but get discouraged if they don't have someone to help them navigate the format. It does take time to learn the ins and outs of the prayer.

Thankfully, technology has made it much easier to pray the Liturgy of the Hours. There are some great apps available that walk you easily through the hours. The app iBreviary loads all the offices of the day and lays them out so you just pray and scroll—no page turning or ribbon adjusting necessary. Universalis is another app that includes the offices but uses a slightly different translation and costs a bit more money. The advantage to Universalis is that you can look ahead to other days and readings, whereas iBreviary will only load the readings of the day. For most people though, iBreviary will be absolutely sufficient to get started with the Liturgy of Hours.

Nevertheless, it is still a great idea to learn how to use the actual print version of the Liturgy of the Hours. There is something very visceral about holding a book of prayer and turning the pages. And there is something very appropriate in having to ask someone to help you learn how to use it, allowing them to guide you, as Christians have guided one another over the centuries in learning this beautiful prayer. Also, praying with a partner and having him or her teach you how to use this book is a great way to build accountability in prayer.

The apps are wonderful, especially if you have no one to teach you, but a priest or deacon or religious sister at your parish might be able to help you learn the ropes in a print edition. Most would be happy and excited to pass on this tradition and invite more people into this great prayer of the Church.

CHAPTER 5

Mary's Scripture Study: The Rosary as the Most Compact Bible Study

The Rosary is one of the most well-known and popular forms of prayer that we have as Catholics. You've probably seen people praying it around your church. You've seen rosary beads hanging on rearview mirrors. You may have received a rosary as a gift at some point. Maybe you pray it often, and maybe you never do, but either way you might wonder: Why do Catholics pray this way? Why not just talk to God? And what's the deal with the beads?

In the early thirteenth century, the Blessed Virgin Mary is said to have appeared to a young Spanish priest we now know as St. Dominic. While the roots of the *rosarium* (Latin word meaning "rose garden") date back even earlier, St. Dominic is credited as being the one who first gave this prayer to the Church, on the expressed wish of Mary, the Mother of God.

Over the centuries, the Rosary has grown into a timeless family prayer, one that has been prayed by billions of souls in languages around the world. At every moment of the day, in almost every conceivable corner of the earth—in homes and in churches, in hospital rooms and in schools, in jail cells and on battlefields—the Catholic faithful join their prayers and dive more deeply into the mysteries of Jesus Christ's life through the Rosary.

If you've never prayed the Rosary or do not do so regularly, you are probably unaware that it is one of the great gifts not only of Catholicism but also of your ongoing Scripture study. The four sets of mysteries—Joyful, Luminous, Sorrowful, and Glorious—will help you focus your prayer on important biblical moments straight from Jesus' and Mary's lives, on truths about God's love for you, and on the meaning of the events in your own life.

Whether prayed individually or in a group, the structure of the Rosary will ask you to come back, again and again, to enter into conversation with God. You'll be invited to "put out into the deep" waters of contemplation and gain new insights into Scripture stories you've heard over and over again, whose truths will never be exhausted. You'll begin to feel God engaging you spiritually, emotionally, mentally, and physically. Each prayer acts as an invitation to become a more perfect disciple, like Mary.

In the sections that follow, I'll give a brief overview of the four sets of mysteries as well as some scriptural citations. Even if you know the stories of the mysteries well, I strongly encourage you to open your own Bible and read them again as if for the first time. Pay attention to the details. Look for action verbs, emotions, locations, numbers, and key characters in each. Remember, no detail is superfluous. The Holy Spirit inspired every word, making it worthy of your contemplation.

Following each citation too, I'll offer a short reflection or series of questions you may want to take to deeper prayer, to journaling, to discussion, or for reference the next time you study the Bible by "rolling the beads" with Mary.

The Joyful Mysteries

At first glance, the Joyful Mysteries might not appear that joyful. Consider these moments from the Gospels: A teenage virgin is pregnant, but not with her husband-to-be's child. The girl then leaves home for three months; later, in her third trimester of pregnancy, she leaves home again and travels ninety miles by donkey. She gives birth in a cave and hears from a prophet that both she and her child will suffer greatly. And then, to top it all off, years later when her son—the Son of God—is a preteen, he goes missing for three days as she and her husband search frantically for him

Most people would not consider these moments very joyful. Prayerful reflection on the mysterious events, however, reveals a cause for intense joy. God was on a rescue mission to save you, and that mission included courageous souls fighting through incredibly challenging situations. Not only do the Joyful Mysteries walk us more deeply into the conception, birth, and childhood years of our Lord Jesus, but they also reveal to us a God who is madly in love with us, a God who will stop at nothing to save all of us from sin and death.

As you reflect on the Joyful Mysteries, you have the opportunity to see the characters from a new point of view. Put yourself into their sandals as they walk. In each mystery, place yourself in the story. Hear their voices. Watch their reactions. See how God's plan to send a Redeemer unfolds.

The Annunciation

Read Luke 1:26–33, 38 and John 1:14.

Mary's *fiat* (meaning "Let it be") is the *yes* that changed the course of human history. Mary's courage teaches us an invaluable lesson: her yes did not mean she was without fear but rather that she trusted God and acted *in spite of* her fear. Courage is not the absence of fear; courage is the refusal to be mastered by fear.

What about you? The God of the universe has great things in store for you. He wants you to do something wonderful for him. Ask him to guide you by his Holy Spirit, and trust that his plan will unfold as you remain attentive and faithful to him. Allow yourself to respond—even if with fear and confusion—as Mary did. Read and highlight **Psalm 56:3.**

Take comfort in the words the angel spoke to Mary, the same message that can be found repeated hundreds of times in Scripture: "Do not be afraid." Open your Bible to **Jeremiah 1:8,** and commit it to memory.

The Visitation

Read Luke 1:39–45.

It is not easy to set aside anxiety and worry in order to celebrate the joy of good news. Fear of the future, broken relationships, financial stress, struggles with work or school, worry about what others think of you—whatever your worries are, they are real and valid, but they needn't strip you of the joy that comes from knowing God.

In this scene, we see a key to living the joy of the gospel. Reread Elizabeth's greeting to her cousin: "Blessed are you who believed that what was spoken to you by the Lord would be fulfilled." Mary traveled *in haste*. Though overwhelmed, I'm sure, Mary went with passion, urgency, and joy to share the good news with her cousin. Despite the very real legal concerns and potential scandal of her situation, she believed that God would honor his promises to her.

What promises has the Lord made to you? Do you believe that the promises that the Lord has spoken to you will be fulfilled? Do you trust that the Lord is with you even when the future is not clear? Ponder **Proverbs 3:5–6** and **Isaiah 41:10.**

The Nativity of Jesus

Read Luke 2:6–20 and Matthew 1:18–25.

When you think of that holy night, how do you see it? Do you tend to idealize it—to imagine it as neat and tidy like the nativity scenes found in your home or parish? Or do you imagine the smells and sounds of the cave in which salvation came into the world?

The physical poverty of the experience (a smelly stable, a manger for a crib, unwashed shepherds as the first guests) is an outward sign of the inward state of the Holy Family's hearts. Their poverty of spirit allows them to think first of God and to depend on him for everything. It's an example to us all.

This poverty of spirit leads them to trust that God will provide for them, as he has promised, even when things aren't going according to their best-laid plans. Do you still trust the Lord when it seems the wheels have come off your life? A broken heart is merely an empty manger. Invite the Virgin and the carpenter to pray beside you. Invite the Savior to dwell there. Ask for the poverty of spirit to think first of God and not yourself. Consider **Matthew 5:3** and **Psalm 132:15** in light of the Eucharist; we are walking mangers for the bread of life.

The Presentation of Jesus

Read Luke 2:22–39.

Do you always recognize Christ?

Simeon's aged eyes were able to clearly recognize Jesus for who he was—his Savior. Just as he did for Simeon, God will open your eyes to a powerful understanding of his mercy. Will you recognize him when he does? What is clouding your vision and preventing you from seeing Jesus not only as healer or teacher but as your Savior?

If you are having trouble seeing Jesus' power and grace working in your life, start with confession. Often sin has obscured our vision and deafened our ears, and we cannot respond to the Lord because of these impediments we ourselves have chosen. Once we have confessed and have returned to a state of grace, we can more easily see the guidance God offers us, especially as we meditate on Scripture.

Pray **Acts 3:19, Luke 6:42,** and **Matthew 5:8.** Proclaim, as Simeon did, through your words and your actions, that the

Lord—who is mercy—is before you. Witness to the God within you so that others might seek to know him too.

The Finding of Jesus

Read Luke 2:41–51.

Can you imagine how you would feel if your only child went missing and, after three days of worry and searching, you found him only to have him greet you with these words: "Why were you looking for me? Did you not know that I must be in my Father's house?"

On the surface, it might seem that Jesus is responding to his parents' concerns with indifference, but there is a key lesson here for us. Jesus understands that his identity as God's Son and his obedience to his heavenly Father's will take precedence over everything else. What if we, in our most dire hour, focused on God's will more than our own? What if—in seeking the Lord—we actually *sought the Lord* and not merely the answers to our own questions?

Ponder this mystery in light of **Psalm 34:4, 1 Samuel 3:10,** and **Isaiah 6:8.**

The Luminous Mysteries

When you look at the world, do you see it as a place of great darkness or tremendous light? When you hear people speak about modern culture, are you filled with hope or despair? Whether you are an optimist or a pessimist, most agree that the world isn't in very good shape these days. War, disease, starvation, natural disasters, and financial problems fill the airwaves and leave many in search of answers, of hope, and ultimately of God.

The Luminous Mysteries extend Christ's invitation to *you* to be a light in the world. As you reflect on them, you'll enter into some of the most miraculous and amazing moments of Christ's life on earth.

You'll be there as the sky rips open during Jesus' baptism. You'll witness water turning to wine. You'll hear Christ's voice announce the kingdom of God with authority. You'll be blinded by the radiance of Jesus transfigured atop a mountain. You'll sit in the Upper Room, consuming the Eucharist as Jesus' love consumes you.

Look deeply into his eyes during every encounter, and watch as his light still illuminates the world—your world—no matter how dark it may seem.

The Baptism of Jesus

Read Matthew 3:11–17 and John 1:26–34.

Do you ever wonder if God loves you—I mean *really* loves you? Do you ever fall into the trap of thinking that God's love for you varies based upon how you act?

Don't. Don't fall into that trap.

Read that line from the Gospel again, "You are my beloved Son; with you I am well pleased" (**Mark 1:11**). God was talking to Jesus, but he offers us too the gift of his love in baptism.

Through the grace of your baptism, you have been claimed and named—you are a son or a daughter of God. Is that too hard to believe, too incredible to grasp? Highlight **Romans 8:15** in your Bible, and pore over those words for a few moments.

Feel the humid air next to the River Jordan while you pray. Listen to the running water. See the dove descend and hear the voice of your heavenly Father reminding you that his love is not conditional; it is perfect. Nothing you do can make God love you more, and nothing you do can make God love you less. Memorize **Romans 5:8, 1 Timothy 1:15,** and **Jeremiah 17:14.**

Our sin affects our ability to receive his love but doesn't do anything to lessen his love for us. And the next time you dip your hand in that holy water and make the Sign of the Cross, remember your baptism, the gift you were given, the water of the Jordan that preceded it, and the fact that the Trinity who was present there is present to you today.

The Miracle at Cana

Read John 2:1–11.

Do you ever feel as if your prayer requests are unimportant or that your life is somehow insignificant? You aren't the first, but you also couldn't be further from the truth. No prayer request, no hope or dream, no concern or anxiety, is insignificant to God. If it matters to you, it matters to the One who created you.

Now, that doesn't mean that we'll get everything that we pray for (that wouldn't be good for us), nor does it mean that everything we stress about is worthy of stress. What it means is that when we go to God, he promises that he listens to us (just check out **Jeremiah 29:12**).

Mary gives us a really important example of humility and of trust at Cana. Mary wasn't trying to manipulate Jesus' power, to get him to reveal it before it was time. This wasn't about trying to change Jesus' mind about how or when to demonstrate his divinity. Mary and Jesus share the same blood and the same heart for their heavenly Father. Mary's petition to Jesus was a prayer of humility. She brought a situation that troubled her to Jesus' attention, and then she trusted that God's will—whatever it was—would happen through Jesus' intercession. Consider her command in **John 2:5.** Do you think of yourself as a servant of the Lord, or do you think of yourself as the one he is to serve?

As Catholics, we are always encouraged to develop the type of relationship with Mary in which we go to her, pray with her, and ask her to pray (intercede) on our behalf to her Son. In honoring her, we obey the Commandments (the fourth, to be specific), and we act as Jesus acted (see **Matthew 11:29**).

If Jesus had declined her request, it would not have meant that Mary was unloved. The fact that Jesus honored Mary's request, though, shows us something about God's heart for her and about the honor she holds in heaven. Read **James 4:10,** and journal about the wisdom found in that handful of words.

The Proclamation of the Kingdom

Read Mark 1:14–15 and Matthew 6:33.

At Mass we often hear that "heaven and earth are filled with his glory." Do you believe that? Is that what you think when you watch the news or scroll through your Twitter feed? Beyond shots of amazing sunsets, how often do you see the glory of God on your Instagram or through a rant on someone's Facebook post?

Is earth really filled with God's glory? Because it can be pretty hard to see it if so. It's in those moments of doubt, however, that we need to look upward (**Romans 1:20**) and inward (**Colossians 1:26–27**).

Catholics are invited to see differently, to be enlightened, to view things from a broader perspective, to see things through Mary's eyes (**Luke 2:19**). Look at the line of sinners wanting to become saints outside the confessional. Look at brides and grooms still wanting to get married in an actual church before an altar of sacrifice, pledging their lives to one another. Look at men lying on their faces, swearing their lives and obedience to the holy priesthood. Look at young women and men peacefully kneeling while making final vows in a religious order. Those people are fulfilling the command our Lord gives us in **Matthew 10:27**.

Consider that, every time you proudly profess your faith in public, lead a prayer before a meal in a restaurant, witness to your love of God online, or reach out to pray with and help a friend in need—in all those times—you are proclaiming the kingdom of God. You are living out your faith with humble boldness and unashamedly announcing to the world that the kingdom of God is at hand!

The Transfiguration

Read Matthew 17:1–8.

Notice that it was only after a long walk up the high mountain that the Lord gave his closest followers a taste of what is to come for all of us, a foreshadowing of the beauty and peace and glory of God that awaits all of us who are willing to follow him. Highlight and memorize **2 Timothy 2:11–12.**

The mountain is important. Why not beside the sea, where so many other teachings and miracles took place? Why not in the boat on the sea, like the others? Perhaps because when scaling a mountain, many things occur. Your perspective changes. Your effort changes. Steps aren't easy; they require effort. Breathing isn't easy; it requires more work. You feel every step, notice every hardship, and have to keep pushing forward. Consider **Matthew 7:7**—all three of Jesus' admonitions have one thing in common: effort on our part.

Climbing the mountain is a great metaphor for the Christian life, because when you keep following the Lord and keep pushing through the journey, you no longer see things the same way. Those problems that seem huge at ground level really aren't so huge any longer; they're tiny. The closer you stay to the Lord and the higher you allow him to take you and call you, the closer you are to heaven.

You have friends, family members, and neighbors who aren't yet walking with Jesus. You have others who are but who still want to remain in the world, feet planted in what is comfortable and popular. You have friends who are following more closely but are not yet ready to fully surrender to Christ; they're camping at the bottom of the mountain.

What about you? Are you living a bold life for Christ? Are you abandoned to all that he wants for you and wants to give you? Is he calling you to scale the mountain behind him? Because you will only see what he wants to reveal once you've left everything else behind and you're following only Christ. Commit **John 6:68** to memory.

The Institution of the Eucharist

Read Matthew 26:26–28 and John 6:33–59.

You have no idea how highly God thinks of you. He created you, yes. He claimed you at your baptism as his son or daughter, of course. He provides for you, blesses you, protects you, and sends people into your life to guide you, absolutely. But have you ever stopped to consider why he gave us the Eucharist?

The God of the universe thinks so highly of you that he allows himself to literally dwell within you. Consider this point in light of **Galatians 2:20.**

He didn't have to do it this way. He could have decided to dwell in you spiritually and leave it at that. It didn't have to be so physical or so tangible. God could have opted not to give us the Eucharist, knowing that many would take this amazing blessing for granted. God loves us so much that he offers us—physical beings—his own physical presence and touch through the sacraments. Read **John 1:14,** and journal about what it is saying in light of this truth.

It's easy to get caught up in the "how" of the Eucharist. How does bread become flesh? How does the wine become his blood? How does the priest fit in with this? But when we ask the *how,* we miss the more important question of *why?*

Why would God choose to do this for us? Why does God humble himself and make himself so available in this way? Why does he command us to do it so often? Maybe, just maybe, God thinks more highly of us than we do of ourselves—and maybe God knows better than we do what we really need. Pray with **Romans 14:7** and **2 Corinthians 5:15–16.**

When we receive the Eucharist, not only are we consuming him, but also he is consuming us with his love. God wants to change us from the inside out. When we receive God's Body and Blood, we receive his very life (called "grace") into our bodies and souls. Just as with the apostles in the Upper Room, this meal changes everything—and it's available to you at every single Mass.

The Sorrowful Mysteries

Part of love is suffering. There is no way around it. While no one likes to suffer, it's a natural part of life (see **John 16:33**). Roses come with thorns. Children come through painful labor. Holy families (as we've seen) deal with hard times. And sometimes we suffer not because God doesn't love us *but because he loves us so much* that he allows us to make our own choices.

Out of all of the mysteries of the Rosary, these are possibly the easiest to visualize. They are physical, tangible, and quite brutal. The Sorrowful Mysteries demonstrate all that is evil in man and all that is beautiful in God.

Have you ever felt abandoned or alone? Our Lord did in the Garden of Gethsemane. Have you ever suffered physical or emotional abuse? Jesus did, and he knows your pain. Have you ever been mocked for who you are or what you believe? Christ was, yet still he loved his enemies.

Have you ever felt that living the Christian life every day was just too difficult? Jesus carried a cross too; even he couldn't escape suffering. Have you ever been humiliated publicly? Our Savior's torment didn't end there. He suffered completely, even unto death, and he did it for you.

Jesus was fully human and fully divine—which means that, at any time, he could have put an end to the suffering he was experiencing. Instead he chose to participate fully in it, experiencing every type of betrayal, desolation, and humiliation you and I could ever feel in life.

You have a Savior who would rather die than risk spending eternity without you.

No suffering can separate you from God (**Romans 8:38–39**). Even death cannot stop God's love.

The Agony in the Garden

Read Luke 22:39–46.

Shortly after supper, Christ and the remaining eleven made their way from the Upper Room to the Garden of Gethsemane, nestled on the Mount of Olives. Just as our relationship with God seemed to have been irreparably damaged in a garden (Eden) by sin, our relationship with God would now be set straight in a garden by grace (see **Romans 5:15–17**).

Our Lord advanced with his three closest disciples and then went further, on his own, to pray. Following God's will is often filled with loneliness, abandonment, suffering, and betrayal. Sadly, it's no walk in a garden. Christ's prayer reminds us that love is far more than a feeling; love is a decision. If true love were only about feelings, Jesus would have been hugged to death for our redemption. Suffering is part of love. The word *passion* comes from the Latin *pati,* which means "to suffer." Ponder the words of **John 3:16, Psalm 9:13,** and **2 Corinthians 12:9.**

Are you *really* giving God permission to have his way with you? Are you willing to endure the moments of doubt regarding your own health, your finances, your job, your marriage, your children, your vocation, and your future? Are you Christ falling on your knees in the Garden of Gethsemane, heralding that the Father's will be done, or are you one of the disciples who fell asleep?[9]

The Scourging at the Pillar

Read Mark 15:6–15.

On most days, our desire to avoid suffering here on earth far outweighs our desire for an existence without suffering in heaven later. We flee from suffering at all costs, and logically so. At the pillar, Jesus offers us a remedial course on love and the suffering that true love often requires. Scripture reminds us that it is through suffering, not through comfort, that we mature in the faith. It's through suffering that we actually grow closest to Christ. Read and then journal about **Romans 5:3; 2 Corinthians 1:5; Philippians 3:10;** and **Colossians 1:24.**

Whether our suffering is physical, emotional, or mental, it is valid, and the Lord—who also suffered—cares not only *for* us but *about* us. If we have the strength to call on the Lord in the midst of our pain, our faith is bolstered. If we trust God our Father and believe that his ultimate goal for us is that heavenly reunion, we will stay on the straight and very narrow path that so many others avoid (**Matthew 7:13–14**).[10]

Journal about **Isaiah 53:5.**

The Crowning with Thorns

Read John 19:1–16.

Mockery and persecution are never far from those who live out the faith. The world criticizes the faithful because they contradict what the world thinks is normal. When people attack you for your beliefs or morals, do not grow weary. The crown of righteousness awaits you (see **2 Timothy 4:8** and **1 Peter 3:14**).

Jesus understood the loneliness that often accompanies those who refuse to bow down to the standards of the world. We must never forget the promise that Christ made to us: "Blessed are those who are persecuted for righteousness' sake, for theirs is the kingdom of heaven" (**Matthew 5:10**). Sometimes God allows suffering as a way to help us grow in virtue (see **James 1:2; 1 Peter 4:3; Romans 5:4**).

Christ's passion reminds us that earthly glory is woven from thorns. That is one reason why we as Catholics embrace a splintered crucifix rather than a shiny cross. There is no Easter Sunday without Good Friday; the beauty of the rose is born from the reality of the thorns. Christ reminded us that if we want to live, we must first learn how to die (see **Luke 9:23–24**)—to sin, to self, and to the world.

The Carrying of the Cross

Read Luke 23:26–32 and John 19:16–22.

Thousands of people, in town for Passover, watched as the convicted "criminal" marched to his death. He had told his apostles of the suffering that awaited him, and Jesus now bore the weight of that cross. The splintered crossbeam dug into his shoulders—the wood stained with the blood of the Lamb (see **Exodus 12:1–12** and **John 1:29**). Though his suffering would bring life, his walk was one of death. Jesus embraced more than the physical pain in that moment. With each step forward, Christ took on our sin. Jesus took our death sentence as his own.

God alone knows your most intimate fears and struggles. Only Christ knows the full weight of the cross you carry each day; only the Lord fully understands the pains or fears you carry deep within. Read and journal about **Hebrews 4:15–16.**

Some crosses appear smaller than others, but everyone has a cross to carry. Go to Jesus with your struggles now. Invite him into your struggle. Pray to him. You are not journeying alone. Trust in the words of **1 John 5:14** and **Psalm 34:15.**

Prayer is where the cross changes shoulders.

The Crucifixion

Read Matthew 27:33–54, Luke 23:33–47, and John 19:25–30.

Contemplate the blood-covered rocks of Golgotha. Salvation is messy; like the flood, sometimes grace comes violently.[11]

The skies have grown dark. Rain falls. The earth quakes. Creation reacts to the loss of its Creator. Evil laughs as the Transfigured One now hangs lifeless and disfigured. The angels remain silent. The Lord let himself be destroyed. No more words. No more miracles. Christ does nothing to save himself, yet he offers everything to save us. It is finished.

Pray with **Philippians 2:8, Colossians 1:20,** and **Hebrews 12:2.**

Picture God's face bloodied and brutalized, his eyes swelled shut, his speech labored, his scalp covered with sacred blood from the earthly crown pressed into his regal head—the very same head that Mary and Joseph kissed long ago beneath the same southern sky of Israel.

Peer into the tortured eyes looking with forgiveness upon his torturers. Hear the voice of the one who once healed with spit but has now been spat upon. Ponder the sinful irony that the carpenter who used tools and wood daily, in peace, is now being destroyed by tools—nails and hammers—and wood. The woodworker is now upon the wood. The Living Water is thirsty. The Good Shepherd has become the Lamb. God is dying not because he lacks an answer to sin but because we did.[12]

Ponder **1 Peter 2:24.** Highlight **Galatians 1:3–5.** Memorize **Galatians 6:14.**

The Glorious Mysteries

Remember, death cannot stop God's love. Our God is a God of life. He came that you would not just have life but have abundant life (**John 10:10**). He came so that you'd enjoy the greatest possible life, and that life is only possible with God. He came to earth to get you to heaven, and that is a glorious thing.

Each glorious mystery reminds us that God our Father doesn't merely keep his promises to us; he exceeds them. Not only did Jesus rise from the dead; his victory offers you the opportunity to live forever. He ascended into heaven, where he now reigns. And as the Bible reminds us, *"If we endure, we shall also reign with him"* (**2 Timothy 2:12**).

When the Holy Spirit descended in power, he gave birth to our Catholic Church and ensured, through the sacraments, that we would never be without Christ. The kingdom of heaven has a headquarters on earth, guaranteeing that we never go without Jesus, who promised to be with us always (**Matthew 28:20**).

One of Jesus' greatest gifts to us is the gift of his own mother (**John 19:26–27**). And in Mary's assumption and coronation as queen of heaven, we are assured that she prays for us and with us. She is calling us to look to her Son, to serve him and him alone.

Heaven exceeds your wildest dreams. Your extended family, the communion of saints, is praying for you and awaiting your arrival. Great things lie ahead! If you open yourself up to the Holy Spirit's power and God's grace, then you too will be a saint. You will be raised up, and that's a promise—his promise.

The Resurrection

Read Mark 16:1–7 and John 20:1–29.

Either he did or he didn't.

That's really what Easter boils down to in the end. Either Jesus rose from the dead or he did not. Regardless of what modern atheists, amateur historians, and questionable cable documentaries want to assert, the question that souls have wrestled with for two thousand years is "Did Jesus Christ really rise from the dead?" The assertion seems preposterous. Preposterous, that is, unless the man in question is also God in the flesh. Do you believe it? Do you *really believe* it?

St. Paul certainly did. Highlight **1 Corinthians 15:14–19, Colossians 3:1,** and **Romans 6:4.** St. Peter knew it to be true as well. Read **1 Peter 1:21** and **Acts 2:32; 3:15.**

Of course, you do too. If you didn't, it's doubtful you'd have made it this far in this book. Sure, the devil may try to distract you (**Romans 7:21**), dissuade you, or cause you to have normal human doubts (**Matthew 28:17**) from time to time, but in your heart of hearts, you know Christ is risen.

Consider this. If Christ did not rise from the dead, an even more extraordinary miracle occurred: eleven random guys pretended he did, having left their families and jobs and traveled to the ends of the earth to teach and baptize in his name—all to protect the greatest lie in history while dying gruesome martyrs' deaths. Still, some modern minds would rather believe that scenario over the simple truth: God came to save us because we could not save ourselves from our sins.

Sometimes the truth sounds almost too good to be true. God died so that we would not have to, and God rose so that we could too. The Lord came to beat death with death (see **Philippians 2:8**) and invites us into eternity with him. Alleluia!

The Ascension of Jesus

Read Luke 24:45–53 and Acts 1:6–11.

Jesus ascends into heaven. The disciples stare blankly into the sky. What in the world just happened? And what in the world does this mean?

The beauty of the Feast of the Ascension lies in the details. First, Jesus ascended to heaven with his glorified body bearing the marks of crucifixion as he took his place on the throne of heaven (see John 20:24–29 for a reference to Jesus carrying his wounds in his glorified body). These wounds remind us that we have a God who understands our suffering, whom we can humbly approach with our needs, in our trials and our joys (see **Hebrews 10:19–24**). Our God understands, and he invites us into this throne room and sanctuary. Jesus' bodily ascension opens the door for our bodily resurrection at the end of time. Ponder **Matthew 17:2, 1 John 3:2,** and **1 Corinthians 15:13–18.**

The second important detail is that Jesus will return with his glorified body in judgment. As the apostles stare at the sky as if they have just seen a double rainbow, an angel tells them that time is limited. They shouldn't "just stand there"—they have work to do in spreading the gospel before Jesus comes again! We have work to do in inviting others to know the God who understands our sufferings and invites us into his mercy.

Plenty of daily missions go unfulfilled. Many followers of Jesus are standing around, heads in the clouds (see the reading from Acts), wondering what to do next. The apostles had an excuse, as they had not yet received the Holy Spirit at Pentecost (that would happen nine days later). You've been baptized, however. You've most likely been confirmed. You're not lacking in the Holy Spirit. Memorize **2 Timothy 1:7.**

So what's your excuse? Are you out proclaiming Christ to the nations? Do others see your bold witness and seek the sacraments that bring you such confidence and joy?

The Descent of the Holy Spirit

Read Acts 2:1–11.

On the Feast of Pentecost, the Jews annually celebrated a harvest festival (see **Exodus 23:16**), celebrating God's fidelity for the bounty he provided through rain, crops, and so on. Additionally (and traditionally), the Feast of Pentecost was closely connected with the Jews' receiving the law of God through Moses atop Mount Sinai.

Just as God overshadowed and touched earth in a powerful way on Mount Sinai, offering truth to his children in an effort to draw all people to himself, now the Holy Spirit overshadows and touches earth with the power of God yet again. The same Spirit who will lead us to all truth (see **John 16:13**) descends not to the mountaintop but to the Upper Room, imparting spiritual gifts to the disciples gathered there, in order to empower them to fulfill their evangelistic mission.

Like this encounter in Acts, a life led by the Holy Spirit is still exciting and "unsafe" today. The apostles were on the verge of changing the world; all they were lacking was the power of God. Christians can and will "renew the face of the earth" (**Psalm 104:30**), and they have for centuries, wherever they have allowed the Spirit to work through them. Pentecost invites us to jump into God's will with total abandon, serving whomever and wherever his love directs us.

Pray with and journal about **2 Corinthians 3:17, Romans 8:14,** and **2 Timothy 1:7.**

The Assumption of Mary

Read Luke 1:46–55 and Revelation 11:19—12:1.

The Bible does not explicitly state that Mary was assumed into heaven, but the Church from early days spoke of this belief—for reasons ranging from its appropriateness, given Mary's role as the mother of Jesus, to the fact that no relics of Mary, neither her body nor her bones, remained to be venerated as relics. The latter is so even though, from the first, the Church collected and honored the remains of its saints and martyrs.

Within a broader context, the Church also sees Mary's assumption indicated in the verses above from Revelation.

This revelation of "the woman" refers to Mary, who is often identified as the new "Ark of the Covenant." We know from **Hebrews 9:4** that the original ark of the covenant—constructed by (or under the direction of) Moses—contained the Ten Commandments (the Law), a pot of manna (the heavenly bread), and the staff of Aaron (a symbol of priesthood). The ark was made to God's exact specifications from the finest, purest materials and was kept free from all defect and corruption.

As the Ark of the *New* Covenant, Mary carried Christ, who is the Law, the Bread of Life, and the royal High Priest (see **Hebrews 5:5, 10**). Her immaculate conception and her ever-virgin state kept her free from defect and sin, preserving her until her earthly life ended. Then she was immediately assumed into heaven, to preserve her from any bodily corruption and foreshadowing our own future glory (**1 Corinthians 15:20–50**).

Similarly, but distinctly, Enoch and Elijah were both assumed into heaven (see **Genesis 5:24; Hebrews 11:5; 2 Kings 2:11–12; 1 Maccabees 2:58**).

Notice too, in this passage from Revelation, that we see the ark (which is missing on earth) in heaven immediately preceding our vision of this woman crowned in stars and holding a baby.

The Coronation of Mary

Read Revelation 12:1–6.

Though Scripture does not have an official "coronation ceremony" for Mary, this scene from Revelation is very close. Given the apocalyptic nature of the writing, the symbolism is being used to evoke and describe a literal truth, namely that Mary sits as queen of heaven and earth.

St. Paul assures us that the saints—and Mary is elevated above every other saint—are "crowned" in righteousness (see 2 **Timothy 4:8**). St. James reminds us about the crown we are promised too (highlight **James 1:12**). Our first pope, St. Peter, discusses the "unfading crown of glory," the right to which, if anyone has a "right" to it, would belong to the one whose *yes* ushered in the conquering of death. We see Christ promising not only new life but the crown of new life (see **Revelation 2:10**), and in the Book of Wisdom, we are reminded of our reward from the Lord (**Wisdom 5:16**).

These verses only serve to corroborate the conclusion that Tradition is correct not only to uplift Mary as queen but also to uphold the ancient tradition, confirmed in her assumption, that Mary was set apart from the beginning.

Don't forget: to whom did God give this vision that we read in Revelation? He imparted it to St. John, the one to whom Jesus entrusted his mother (see **John 19:26–27**) for the remainder of her days on earth. It seems fitting that the "disciple whom Jesus loved," who had a stronger and longer connection to Mary than any of the other apostles, would be given even more intimate knowledge as to her elevated and regal role within the communion of saints.

Well, there you have it. Twenty mysteries and over one hundred biblical citations to guide your prayer in order to deepen your appreciation of the Rosary and Sacred Scripture. The more we dive into the word with the contemplative heart of Mary, the more these passages and scenes will come to life in our lives.

As you pray too, you will begin to see just how deeply intertwined different passages and books are, even if separated by decades and centuries. In the timeless mind and heart of God, all things are present.

CHAPTER 6

Through Him, with Him, and in Him: Scripture as the Foundation of the Mass

Thunder and lightning crash out of the clouds of smoke that surround the mountaintop. Flames wreathe the summit, and a trumpet blast shakes the very ground on which you stand. The people around you cower and shake, awestruck at the spectacle taking place. Suddenly a figure emerges—a prophet—and begins to speak words given by God himself. A voice cuts through the cacophony of thunder and the crackle of fire and proclaims:

"Thus says the Lord!"

Similar scenes play out numerous times in Sacred Scripture. God's voice is heard amid fantastic visuals that signal his presence. Prophets can be foreboding characters, proclaiming mercy for sinners and judgment for the self-righteous. As mouthpieces of the Divine, they bear the burden of responsibility for carrying the word of God, and they do so with great care and solemnity.

My guess is that the last time you heard Scripture proclaimed at Mass, you had a slightly different experience from the one described above.

The creaking of pews and shuffling of missalette pages awkwardly cuts through the muffled coughs of the 7:00 a.m. congregation. Members of the community gaze off into the distance, wishing they had consumed another cup of coffee before coming to church that morning. A few look through the bulletin as a figure makes his way to the lectern and accidentally strikes the microphone with the Lectionary. The "pop" startles some of the congregation awake and elicits grunts from others. A voice cuts through the silence, stumbling through the names of forgotten cities with the gusto of a disgruntled worker at a government office. At the end, and almost as an afterthought, a voice wobbles through the stale morning air:

"The Word of the Lord."

And the murmured response:

"Thanks be to God."

This scene is challenging but all too common. The author of the Letter to the Hebrews says that the word of God is "living and active, sharper than any two-edged sword, piercing to the division of soul and spirit, of joints and marrow, and discerning the thoughts and intentions of the heart" (**Hebrews 4:12**). That's an intense description for Sacred Scripture, yet we seem to meet the word of God with a surprising amount of apathy when we hear it proclaimed.

It doesn't have to be this way, however. While we may not be able to change the tenor of the lector or the vigor of the rest of the congregation, we can change our hearts. The power of the word of God doesn't depend on the person speaking it; it is powerful in itself. It can transform our hearts, but we must let it. The beautiful truth of the Mass is that, when we enter into it, we don't just get Scripture for half of the Mass, during the Liturgy of the Word; we get Scripture throughout the entire Mass, beginning to end.

Steeped in Scripture

As we've discussed, Catholics are often accused of not knowing as much about the Bible as our Protestant brothers and sisters. There is some (sad) truth to this statement; many Catholics don't know Sacred Scripture as well as they should. However, to say that Catholicism as a whole doesn't appreciate or know the Bible is just misleading. The Mass, our highest form of worship, is saturated in Sacred Scripture.

As you begin to dive deeper into the word of God, you'll notice that many of our responses, prayers, and actions during the liturgy either come directly from the pages of the Bible or are based on biblical phrases and passages. Knowing where these lines come from and their context will not only deepen your love for the Mass but increase your love for the Bible as well.

It makes sense that many of the words and actions found in Sacred Scripture would be part of our Mass. After all, the Mass has roots in the Old Testament—for example, the Passover meal, as described in Exodus 12 and as celebrated by Jesus with his apostles—and predates the development of the New Testament. The early Christian Church celebrated the Eucharistic liturgy (the Mass) very soon after Jesus' death and resurrection, in accordance with his command (**Luke 22:19–20**). Understanding these biblical roots will help us enter into the heavenly movements of the Mass and make us better able to appreciate what we are being invited into every single Sunday (and every weekday too).

Introductory Rites

The gathering rites for Mass begin, in a sense, before we even set foot in the church. God calls us to worship, and this call to worship is reflected throughout Sacred Scripture. People assemble for many things—sports, concerts, family gatherings with bad food—but when people assemble to pray and worship God, something different is happening. It is God himself who calls the assembly. Throughout the Old Testament, this kind of assembly is called a *qahal*, a special gathering of people who come together specifically to worship. The exodus from Egypt really was about the right to gather for worship, something that happens in Exodus 19 when the people form a *qahal* to receive the covenantal law. The word *qahal* later is translated into Greek as *ekklesia*, which we translate into English as "church."

The gathering rite begins with the Sign of the Cross, which acknowledges to whom we belong and the sign by which we are saved. When we make the Sign of the Cross, we remember that we are bought with a price (**1 Corinthians 6:20**) and are saved through the cross (**1 Corinthians 1:18**). We sign ourselves "in the name of the Father, and of the Son, and of the Holy Spirit," a formula given to the disciples before Jesus' ascension into heaven (**Matthew 28:19**).

The priest offers a greeting from **2 Corinthians 13:14:** "The grace of our Lord Jesus Christ, and the love of God, and the communion of the Holy Spirit be with you all," and we respond using St. Paul's words in **Galatians 6:18,** "And with your Spirit."

Penitential Rite and Gloria

True worship requires humility—the virtue that allows us to acknowledge that God is the Creator and we are not. If we don't humble ourselves, then we can't worship something greater than ourselves. Because humility is the foundation of prayer and worship, we begin Mass by doing something very humbling—calling to mind our sin.

We ask God for mercy because only he, our Creator, can restore us to a right relationship. As we pray, we imitate the prayer of the tax collector in **Luke 18:9–14,** striking our chest, acknowledging that we have "greatly sinned," and asking God for mercy (**Matthew 15:22; 17:15**). This plea for mercy is found throughout the Bible. It keeps us humble and allows us to enter into worship with the correct mind-set.

During Mass on a Sunday or major feast day, we pray the Gloria, a prayer of praise to God. Scripture records numerous instances of a prophet having a vision of heavenly worship. Isaiah and Ezekiel, for example, speak notably of visions of angels worshiping God in heaven. Luke also shares a vision of heavenly worship, but this vision is given to shepherds. The opening line of the Gloria comes from this revelation: "Glory to God in the highest" (**Luke 2:14**).

The Gloria reminds us that we aren't worshiping alone, but we are praising God along with the angels and saints in heaven. The rest of the Gloria is taken from other visions of heavenly worship found in the Book of Revelation (**7:12, 19:6**) and various praises and titles given to Christ throughout the letters and Gospels of the New Testament (**2 John 3:8; John 1:29; 14:26; Romans 8:34; Luke 1:32; 4:34**, to name a few).

The Liturgy of the Word

The Liturgy of the Word offers the most obvious connection to Sacred Scripture in the Mass. Depending on whether it's a Sunday, major feast day, or weekday Mass, two or three readings are proclaimed as well as a psalm (or other song from Scripture); all of these are found in a collection called the Lectionary. The Lectionary is broken down into three yearly cycles lettered A, B, and C. The readings are arranged and chosen intentionally to reflect certain themes that match various liturgical seasons. You will notice that as we get closer to the season of Advent (and the end of the liturgical year), the readings focus more on the end times and the second coming of Christ. The readings in Advent lead up to the birth of Christ. During Lent, our readings turn toward the final teachings and days of Jesus.

Readings and Homily

The first reading and the Gospel always share a strong connection. Generally, the first reading is from the Old Testament. This intentional connection shows the continuity between God's plan in the Old Testament and God's plan in the New

Testament. A notable exception occurs during the Easter season, when the first reading often comes from the Acts of the Apostles.

After the first reading, we have the "responsorial." This is usually taken from the Book of Psalms, but as noted, there are occasions when another song from Sacred Scripture may be read (or sung). The next reading on a Sunday or feast day is from one of the letters found in the New Testament. These letters contain insight into Christ's life and teaching and into how we live as Christians. The final reading is always from a Gospel.

The homily following the readings helps us connect the dots and gain important insights about how we can apply God's word in our lives (**2 Timothy 3:16–17**).

Creeds and Petitions

At the conclusion of the homily, we recite either the Nicene Creed or the Apostles' Creed (usually the former). This ancient expression of faith links us to the Church through the ages and expresses who we are and what we believe as Christians. It is a public proclamation of our hope (**1 Peter 3:15**). It begins with the words "I believe," an important profession of faith for every Catholic (**Mark 9:24; John 11:27; John 14:1; 1 John 5:10**).

Our prayers of petition are crucial. We lift up our needs, globally and locally, because we believe that prayer changes hearts, situations, and our world (**Ephesians 6:18; 1 Timothy 2:1**).

The Liturgy of the Eucharist

At this point, you probably see a bit of a theme. Sacred Scripture is woven into the very fabric of the Mass and always points to the deeper spiritual reality that is occurring. Nothing is "just because" or haphazard. Nowhere is this truer than during the Liturgy of the Eucharist.

By now we've humbled ourselves, been nourished by the very word of God, proclaimed who we are, and prayed for our world. The time has come to enter into something incredible: Jesus Christ, our King, will be present among us within the Eucharist. We begin by presenting simple gifts—bread and wine—to be consecrated. These are the same gifts the high priest Melchizedek offered after Abram won a great military victory (**Genesis 14:18**). The priest praises God for the gifts, and we respond by proclaiming, "Blessed be God forever" (**Genesis 14:20**).

As the Eucharistic prayers begin, the congregation says or sings, "Holy, Holy, Holy, Lord God of Hosts," the song sung by angels in the presence of God (**Isaiah 6:3; Revelation 4:8**). The second half of the prayer comes from Jesus' entry into Jerusalem before Passover. The crowds shout, "Blessed is he who comes in the name of the Lord" (**Mark 11:9; Matthew 21:9; Luke 19:38; John 12:13**), quoting a psalm (**Psalm 118:26**). They cry out, "Hosanna in the highest" (**Mark 11:10**), praising Jesus as he enters Jerusalem. We make the same proclamation, because we know that we are entering into the throne room of heaven as the priest asks the Holy Spirit to transubstantiate the gifts of bread and wine into the Body, Blood, Soul, and Divinity of Christ.

There are several options a priest can choose from when it comes to prayers during this part of the Mass. One of the most commonly used (and also the shortest) is Eucharistic Prayer II, which contains an interesting line. The priest asks the Holy Spirit to come upon the gifts "like the dewfall." It seems out of place: why are we talking about early morning moisture in the middle of Mass? Well, it goes back to (you guessed it) the Bible, specifically the Exodus. God gave the Israelites miraculous bread called manna to eat when they were in the desert. When did this heavenly bread show up? Every morning with the dewfall (**Numbers 11:9**). These words call to mind the ways that God fed his people then and the way he is about to feed us with the Eucharist during Mass.

The priest invites the Holy Spirit to make Christ present using words almost exclusively from Sacred Scripture. The most important part of this prayer—the words of institution—are directly from Christ and cannot be changed in any way. These words first appear (chronologically) in **1 Corinthians 11:23–25**, which was written around AD 50. The first Gospel was written shortly after, but St. Paul was actually the first to put down these words, which were already well known because they were spoken at every Mass during the Liturgy of the Eucharist.

Jesus' words, "Take this, all of you, and eat of it, for this is my Body, which will be given up for you," are taken from **Mark 14:22, Matthew 26:26, Luke 22:19,** and **1 Corinthians**

11:24. The second prayer over the chalice, "Take this, all of you, and drink from it, for this is the chalice of my Blood, the Blood of the new and eternal covenant, which will be poured out for you and for many for the forgiveness of sins," is taken from **Mark 14:24, Matthew 26:27–28, Luke 22:17, 20,** and **1 Corinthians 11:25.**

The final statement, "Do this in memory of me," is only found in **Luke 22:19 and 1 Corinthians 11:24–25** ["Do this in remembrance of me"] and deserves some explanation. Many see it as justification of the erroneous view that Jesus' command at the Last Supper makes the Eucharist purely symbolic. Our contemporary understanding is that when we "remember" something, we don't relive it, we simply recall it. But this represents a misunderstanding of how Jesus (and ancient Jews) viewed time. Jesus instituted the Eucharist (and the priesthood) on the night of Passover. This was one of the most important festival times for the Jewish people, because it represented the Exodus from Egypt and God's establishing a covenant with Moses and the Israelites. It was instituted as a celebration that needed to continue "for ever" (**Exodus 12:24**).

When the meal was celebrated, however, it was understood that something spiritually powerful was happening. The people weren't simply "remembering" the Exodus, as though they were recalling it in their minds. They were participating in it. As they read the words of the Book of Exodus and prayed, they were making the journey with the Israelites. Remembering, in this sense, means putting something back together and living it again.

Jesus instituted the Eucharist on Passover to tie into this mentality. When we celebrate the Eucharist, we remember the night before Jesus died and are spiritually transported there as well.

The Lord's Prayer and the Sign of Peace

When Christ is present in the Eucharist following the words of consecration, we enter into the Lord's Prayer and the sign of peace, the part of the Mass that separates those who enjoy holding hands from those who don't and those who give out hugs from those who hold up two fingers in the classic V-for-peace sign. Both the Lord's Prayer and the sign of peace are biblical.

Jesus gave the Lord's Prayer to his disciples in response to their request to "teach us to pray" (**Luke 11:1**). The prayer is an expression of unity and is unique to the Christian community. It is recited at every Mass and can be found in **Matthew 6:9–13.**

As the congregation concludes the Our Father, the priest asks the Lord to deliver us from all evil, and we reply, "For the kingdom, the power, and the glory are yours, now and forever," words reflected in **Revelation 1:6; 4:11; 5:13.** The sign of peace (or what was called the kiss of peace in the early Church) challenges us to recognize that the peace that Christ gives is different from the peace the world gives (**John 16:33**). Jesus often extended a sign of peace to his disciples, and we imitate that action (**John 14:27**).

Prayers before Communion

The sign of peace concludes with the congregation proclaiming, "Lamb of God, you take away the sins of the world, have mercy on us." This line, rooted in **Revelation 5:6–13** and **22:1–3,** is again from a vision of heavenly worship. Grab your Bible, and pray through it. Jesus is the Lamb of God (as identified early on by John the Baptist in **John 1:29**), and he is worshiped eternally by saints and angels. That same Lamb of God is present on our altar, and we offer worship and once more implore mercy.

This is far beyond what we may have once thought "boring," and it unfolds at every Mass. We are called to the wedding feast of the Lamb, and if that isn't explicit enough, the priest makes sure we know it by holding up the Blessed Sacrament and proclaiming, "Behold the Lamb of God, behold him who takes away the sins of the world. Blessed are those called to the supper of the Lamb," which echoes the words of John the Baptist in **John 1:29** and the vision in **Revelation 19:9.**

We respond with the words of the centurion who begged Jesus for healing: "Lord, I am not worthy that you should enter under my roof, but only say the word and my soul shall be healed" (**Matthew 8:8**). You can read the whole story in **Matthew 8:5–13** and be inspired by the centurion's trust that Jesus could heal, even from a distance. Our prayer is an act of both humility and faith and marks one final movement of our heart before we receive Christ in the Eucharist.

Concluding Rites

We gather to be sent. As we conclude Mass, our final prayers and blessings come from Old Testament blessings found in **Genesis 28:3, Deuteronomy 14:29,** and **Numbers 6:23–27.** We are dismissed to bring Christ out into the world, strengthened by the Word and the Sacrament. Just as Jesus sent the disciples in **Matthew 28:19–20,** promising to be with them always, we also trust that Christ will be with us as we go through the week.

It is the same in any Mass you attend, in any Catholic parish, anywhere in the world. It doesn't matter if the music is good or bad or if you "got something" out of the homily. Of course, if we are responsible for serving in any part of the Mass, we should strive to do our best, but we also need to recognize the greater spiritual reality that happens regardless of the human aspects of the liturgy. Understanding the Bible and the ways in which Sacred Scripture is incorporated into the Mass can help us do that and is vital for us as Catholics. Those words don't change, so even if everything else is not handled well, the words still call our minds to what is really happening. We are called to the wedding feast of the Lamb, and we receive our Lord. Blessed are we to be there, let alone to be sent forth to proclaim the good news for the rest of the week.

We are sent forth not as singular souls but as a Church—living and dynamic, filled by the grace of God and inspired by the word of God, "living and active" (**Hebrews 4:12**). The same Spirit who inspired the Scriptures propels and safeguards the Church, because as we have discussed, the Church did not "come out" of the Bible; the Bible came out of the Church.

CHAPTER 7

It's in Your Hands: A Ten-Step Plan to Start Reading Scripture

I encounter thousands of people at different events each year. Most of them are Catholic Christians who want to begin reading the Bible but don't know where to start. If you've read and prayed through this book so far, I hope you too are hungry to dive into Scripture on your own. In this chapter, I've pulled together my advice in order to offer ten tips that will help you do so.

As with anything else, if you want to build something—in this case, your knowledge and love for the Scriptures—you don't just grab a hammer and nails and start pounding. To ensure that you don't jump into reading the Bible and then quit out of frustration or confusion, there are certain things you can do to be more successful.

We'll approach this on three levels—the *tools*, the *blueprint*, and the *construction*. Together, these "steps" will help you build your bodily temple into a biblical fortress, able to resist anything the devil can throw at you (**1 Peter 5:8**).

The Tools

1. Pick a time to read and study, but not just *any* time. Commit to a time, daily, when you will open God's word and pray with it. That being said, be sure to choose a reasonable time.

You know what that means: if you tend to be really tired at the end of the day and can't wait to fall asleep every night, then deciding to read the Bible when you're finally getting into bed probably isn't the best choice.

Pick a time of day when you are totally awake and can give your full attention to what you're doing. This means eliminating all distractions, including screens (unless, of course, you're reading Scripture on your screen). It will most certainly mean putting off other things, getting up earlier, or taking your Bible along with you to work or to school. In every case, be sure to set an alarm on your phone or at your bedside for the same time each day. Virtue is rooted in habit, and consistency is the key to success.

2. Choose a Bible that is functional and offers additional information. Of course, you'll want to have a Catholic Bible with all seventy-three books (forty-six Old Testament, twenty-seven New Testament), but if you don't have a Catholic Bible right now, that shouldn't keep you from reading. Make it your goal, however, to get an actual (non-digital) study Bible with quality Catholic footnotes and commentary. You'll most likely want either the *New American Bible*, which is the version proclaimed at Mass, or the *Revised Standard Version: Catholic Edition*. The *Jerusalem Bible* is another good Catholic translation.

It's important that the Bible is one you're comfortable with, is light enough to take with you on the go, is durable enough that you can really use it, and is inexpensive enough that you don't feel bad writing in it.

Like a telescope, a Bible is only useful if looked *through* not looked *at*. If the only Bible you own is a precious family heirloom or some oversized hardback edition, it's time to choose functionality over sentimentality. The Bible is meant to be used, not admired. Get yourself a good solid paperback you can throw in your backpack, keep in your car, or have on your nightstand.

3. Acquire other books that help you understand *the* Book. There are great resources out there designed to help you understand the Bible better. (I pray you consider this one of them.) I've included a list in the appendix of ancillary materials from highly respected and orthodox authors. Additionally, a host of resources are now available online or as free podcasts or reasonably priced video series (which I also list). Finally, and importantly, it's great to have the *Catechism of the Catholic Church* handy, to refer to as you study.

Okay, so now you have some of the tools. Next, let's get to the blueprint—three things you can do as you begin your study.

The Blueprint (The Pattern You Will Follow)

4. Pray, and then pray some more. You're awake and alert; you have your Bible and some other resources at your fingertips. Before you open God's word, ask the author of that word, the Holy Spirit, to be present in a bold and fierce way. Quiet yourself, spend some time in silence, and *hold the Bible in your hands* as you pray. Ask God, through the power of his Spirit, to open your eyes, your mind, and your heart to his truth. Thank him for the gift of his word, a gift that millions have given their lives to defend and that you have the freedom to read.

This doesn't have to be a long prayer, but take time to do this essential step in Bible study. It's the most important step but too often, it's overlooked or rushed through. A prayerful understanding of the Bible is a key that unlocks many doors—including the doors to your personal spiritual prisons.

5. Have a plan. As you may have gathered while moving through this book, if you were intending to read the Bible cover to cover, don't—or at least not yet. The Bible isn't a novel and was never designed to be read cover to cover, from Genesis straight through to Revelation. After you have studied it for a while, if you want to go back and read it cover to cover, go for it. Until then, you'd be wise to approach the Bible from a different angle.

Pick one book, and make that book your focus for a while. If you're starting from scratch, I'd suggest a Gospel, specifically the Gospel of Mark, which is straightforward and simple. You already know the basic gist of the story, the cast of characters, and the general movement toward the passion and resurrection.

I also strongly recommend the Letter of James as a good place to develop a rhythm of reading. I've heard others recommend Paul's letters, provided that you start with Thessalonians or Philippians or Corinthians. Romans—St. Paul's magnum opus—is a gorgeous and extraordinarily well-written book, but it's too theologically dense for the biblical novice. Romans teaches us how to get to heaven, while James teaches us how to live on earth (with people who might annoy us, for example, and try our patience). James is a great read, only five chapters long and filled with practical insights.

Truthfully, though, you don't have to do a study of a book. You can start with the Mass readings of the day, available on many Catholic apps and in periodicals like *The Word Among Us*. You might also choose to use the passages in the Liturgy of the Hours, the universal daily prayer of the Church that we discussed in chapter four.

6. Get the background for what you are going to study. Don't jump into a letter of St. Paul without learning some of the backstory: To whom is he writing? Why? What's going on in their city? If you are reading the work of a prophet, learn something about his world at the time he was pursuing his ministry. If you choose a Gospel, what are basic themes the author develops? Who is his audience? What makes that specific account different from the others? The resources recommended in the appendix will go a long way in helping you mine the *context* from the overwhelming *content* of your Bible.

Finally, let's go over four things you should remember while reading Scripture and beyond.

The Construction

7. Less is more, in terms of the number of verses you read. Don't just open to the Gospel and read until you get tired, or for fifteen minutes because that's what you committed to doing. Most Bibles break the chapters into smaller sections with headings. If you begin with the first chapter of the Gospel of Mark, for instance, you shouldn't start with verse 1 and plow through to verse 45 (the end of the chapter). Instead, take verses 1 through 8, and spend fifteen minutes meditating on them. The next day, take verses 9 through 11 and ruminate (chew) through them. That first chapter with its 45 verses could be broken down into six to ten different studies alone.

Studying the Scriptures is not like driving across the country—it's not about how much distance you cover in a set amount of time. Roll down the windows, take everything in, and enjoy the ride.

8. Periods are there for a reason. The period at the end of each sentence is a gift. Each little "dot" is an invitation to take a breath and reflect on what you just read and prayed. It's an invitation to consider the smaller picture. At each period, take a moment to envision the story that is unfolding. We discussed this earlier in the book, but it bears repeating: pay attention to detail and let the story come to life.

Here are questions and suggestions to consider as you read Sacred Scripture, limiting yourself to a few verses at a sitting (point #7) and pausing at periods (#8).

Ask yourself such questions as

- Who is involved in this story?
- Who is speaking, and to whom is he or she speaking?

- What's being said? Why?
- What's the main point of the verses?

This might involve reading the footnotes and asking further questions. All the more reason to focus on just a few verses at a time and to pause at periods.

Other questions to consider:

- Where am I in the Bible right now—in other words, at what point in biblical history? (Understanding something of the historical era helps us understand the context.)
- Is God speaking, or is someone else?
- If there are people featured in the verses, are they friends or enemies, receptive to or uninterested in whatever is taking place?
- Why were these verses important then, and why are they important now?
- Do these verses apply to my life today? How does this truth challenge me to live differently?

You might not immediately know the answer to each of these questions, but the more information you have, the less likely you are to get confused or distracted.

Some suggestions to help you put yourself in the picture:

- If you are reading about the baptism of Jesus (**Mark 1:9–11**), don't just say, "Hey, cool, Jesus is getting baptized." Go deeper. Put yourself more intentionally into the story. This is where the elements we discussed in lectio divina can come into play. At his baptism, where are you? Are you on the shore of the Jordan? Are you on the mountain overlooking the scene or in the water right next to Christ? Is the weather hot? Does the water smell? Are there any insects buzzing around? Is it noisy or peaceful? Let the story come alive.

- Look for details in the passage. For example, does the passage mention the time of day, what the scene looked like, or anything that gives you a mental picture? Check out the details St. Mark gives in the following passages: **Mark 1:32–33; 4:35–38; 5:2–5; 6:39–40.** His details give the reader a visual.

- Pay attention to numbers, emotions, icons, and symbols. Were the people angry, confused, overjoyed, afraid, or emotional in any other way? Again, read through these passages from St. Mark's Gospel, and note the points he makes about people's emotional responses: **1:40–41; 3:1–5; 10:13–16; 14:33–34.**

- Pay attention to names, locations, colors, and verb choice. These details are important because sometimes they lend credibility to a passage, remind us of another passage, or communicate the passion and depth of a scene. I encourage you to take the time to pay attention.

9. Use a journal. When verses confuse you or difficult questions arise, write them down in a journal. Don't allow yourself to get hung up on tough verses. Scribble down the verse number with a question mark before moving on. Later, you can search footnotes, books, or websites or ask a person who is knowledgeable about the Bible for more help. The journal isn't just for questions, however. You should also use it to note the images, reflections, consolations, or challenges God gives you and to write out the key verses that stand out for you or spiritually "afflict" you a bit.

10. Put the Book down, *often*. Don't become a bookworm, never taking your eyes off the page. The Bible is the *living Word* (**John 1:1–5; Hebrews 4:12**). It lives and breathes well beyond the page that contains it. Share what you learn. Copy passages and post them around your home, in your car, and, depending on your circumstances, in your office. Send verses to people via text. Post online verses that touch your heart. As with the Eucharist, the word should be taken, blessed, broken (down), and *shared*. The greatest gift you can give someone is to live a life that mirrors the Gospels, reflecting God in all you do. The second greatest gift is to invite others to peer into the mirror of the good news.

In Conclusion

Okay, that's a substantial enough start. Get the tools, pull together your blueprints, and start building your love for God's word. Begin reading Scripture, and keep reading it daily.

And remember, you don't have to "study" every time you open the Bible. Yes, you want to set aside time every day to do that, but consider this: the next time you're waiting in line, eating alone, or stuck at the DMV renewing your license, you can take that time to dip into other biblical books, such as Psalms, Proverbs, Sirach, Wisdom, Ecclesiastes, or Paul's epistles. You'll be blessed by every moment you give to the Lord, opening yourself to him as you open his Word.

All I can tell you, from my own experience, is that the word of God has changed my life. It has deepened my experience of the Eucharist, both at Mass and in Adoration. It has deepened my love for our mother Mary and my gratitude for intercessory prayer and the communion of saints. It has deepened my love for the Church, the papacy, and basic human dignity. It has fueled a fire within me for truth and the need to proclaim it, defend it, and uphold it, especially in our morally relativistic culture.

My deepest and most sincere prayer is that it will do the same for you.

May God bless you always and all ways. Now, get reading!

APPENDIX 1

Three-Year Cycle of Sunday Readings

Year A

Cycle of Sunday readings
2017, 2020, 2023, 2026, 2029

Advent Season

1st Sunday of Advent
1- Isa 2:1–5
2- Rom 13:11–14
Gospel- Mt 24:37–44

2nd Sunday of Advent
1- Isa 11:1–10
2- Rom 15:4–9
Gospel- Mt 3:1–12

3rd Sunday of Advent
1- Isa 35:1–6, 10
2- Jms 5:7–10
Gospel- Mt 11:2–11

4th Sunday of Advent
1- Isa 7:10–14

2- Rom 1:1–7
Gospel- Mt 1:18–24

Christmas Season

Christmas Vigil
1- Isa 62:1–5
2- Acts 13:16–17, 22–25
Gospel- Mt 1:1–25 or 1:18–25

Christmas (at Midnight)
1- Isa 9:1–6
2- Ti 2:11–14
Gospel- Lk 2:1–14

Christmas (at Dawn)
1- Isa 62:11–12
2- Ti 3:4–7
Gospel- Lk 2:15–20

Christmas (during the Day)
1- Isa 52:7–10
2- Heb 1:1–6
Gospel- Jn 1:1–18 or 1:1–5, 9–14

Sunday After Christmas (Holy Family)
1- Sirach 3:2–6, 12–14
2- Col 3:12–21
Gospel- Mt 2:13–15, 19–23

January 1 (Solemnity of Mary, Mother of God)
1- Num 6:22–27
2- Gal 4:4–7
Gospel- Lk 2:16–21

2nd Sunday After Christmas
1- Sirach 24:1–2, 8–12
2- Eph 1:3–6, 15–18
Gospel- Jn 1:1–18 or 1:1–5, 9–14

Epiphany
1- Isa 60:1–6
2- Eph 3:2–3a, 5–6
Gospel- Mt 2:1–12

Sunday After Epiphany (Baptism of the Lord)
1- Isa 42:1–4, 6–7
2- Acts 10:34–38
Gospel- Mt 3:13–17

Lenten Season

Ash Wednesday
1- Joel 2:12–18
2- 2 Cor 5:20—6:2
Gospel- Mt 6:1–6, 16–18

1st Sunday of Lent
1- Gen 2:7–9; 3:1–7

2- Rom 5:12–19 or 5:12, 17–19
Gospel- Mt 4:1–11

2nd Sunday of Lent
1- Gen 12:1–4a
2- 2 Tm 1:8b–10
Gospel- Mt 17:1–9

3rd Sunday of Lent
1- Ex 17:3–7
2- Rom 5:1–2, 5–8
Gospel- Jn 4:5–42 or 4:5–15, 19b–26, 39a, 40–42

4th Sunday of Lent
1- 1 Sam 16:1b, 6–7, 10–13a
2- Eph 5:8–14
Gospel- Jn 9:1–41 or 9:1, 6–9, 13–17, 34–38

5th Sunday of Lent
1- Ezek 37:12–14
2- Rom 8:8–11
Gospel- Jn 11:1–45 or 11:3–7, 17, 20–27, 33b–45

Passion Sunday (Palm Sunday)
Procession: Mt 21:1–11
1- Isa 50:4–7
2- Phil 2:6–11
Gospel- Mt 26:14—27:66 or 27:11–54

Easter Triduum and Easter Season

Holy Thursday, Chrism Mass

1- Isa 61:1–3a, 6ab, 8b–9
2- Rev 1:5–8
Gospel- Lk 4:16–21

Holy Thursday, Mass of the Lord's Supper

1- Ex 12:1–8, 11–14
2- 1 Cor 11:23–26
Gospel- Jn 13:1–15

Good Friday

1- Isa 52:13—53:12
2- Heb 4:14–16; 5:7–9
Gospel- Jn 18:1—19:42

Easter Vigil

1- Gen 1:1—2:2 or 1:1, 26–31a
Gen 22:1–18 or 22:1–2, 9, 10–13, 15–18
Ex 14:15—15:1
Isa 54:5–14
Isa 55:1–11
Baruch 3:9–15, 32—4:4
Ezek 36:16–28
2- Rom 6:3–11
Gospel- Mt 28:1–10

Easter Sunday
1- Acts 10:34a, 37–43
2- Col 3:1–4
or 1 Cor 5:6b–8
Gospel- Jn 20:1–9 or Mt 28:1–10
Evening: Gospel- Lk 24:13–35

2nd Sunday of Easter
1- Acts 2:42–47
2- 1 Pt 1:3–9
Gospel- Jn 20:19–31

3rd Sunday of Easter
1- Acts 2:14, 22–33
2- 1 Pt 1:17–21
Gospel- Lk 24:13–35

4th Sunday of Easter
1- Acts 2:14a, 36–41
2- 1 Pt 2:20b–25
Gospel- Jn 10:1–10

5th Sunday of Easter
1- Acts 6:1–7
2- 1 Pt 2:4–9
Gospel- Jn 14:1–12

6th Sunday of Easter
1- Acts 8:5–8, 14–17
2- 1 Pt 3:15–18
Gospel- Jn 14:15–21

Ascension of Our Lord
1- Acts 1:1–11
2- Eph 1:17–23
Gospel- Mt 28:16–20

7th Sunday of Easter
1- Acts 1:12–14
2- 1 Pt 4:13–16
Gospel- Jn 17:1–11a

Pentecost Vigil
1- Gen 11:1–9
or Ex 19:3–8a, 16–20b
or Ezek 37:1–14
or Joel 3:1–5
2- Rom 8:22–27
Gospel- Jn 7:37–39

Mass of the Day
1- Acts 2:1–11
2- 1 Cor 12:3b–7, 12–13
Gospel- Jn 20:19–23

Solemnities of the Lord During Ordinary Time

Trinity Sunday (Sunday after Pentecost)

1- Ex 34:4b–6, 8–9
2- 2 Cor 13:11–13
Gospel- Jn 3:16–18

Corpus Christi

1- Deut 8:2–3, 14b–16a
2- 1 Cor 10:16–17
Gospel- Jn 6:51–58

Sacred Heart of Jesus (Friday after Corpus Christi)

1- Deut 7:6–11
2- 1 Jn 4:7–16
Gospel- Mt 11:25–30

Ordinary Time

1st Sunday (See Baptism of the Lord, above)

2nd Sunday

1- Isa 49:3, 5–6
2- 1 Cor 1:1–3
Gospel- Jn 1:29–34

3rd Sunday

1- Isa 8:23b—9:3
2- 1 Cor 1:10–13, 17
Gospel- Mt 4:12–23 or 4:12–17

4th Sunday
1- Zeph 2:3; 3:12–13
2- 1 Cor 1:26–31
Gospel- Mt 5:1–12a

5th Sunday
1- Isa 58:7–10
2- 1 Cor 2:1–5
Gospel- Mt 5:13–16

6th Sunday
1- Sirach 15:15–20
2- 1 Cor 2:6–10
Gospel- Mt 5:17–37 or 5:20–22a, 27–28, 33–34a, 37

7th Sunday
1- Lev 19:1–2, 17–18
2- 1 Cor 3:16–23
Gospel- Mt 5:38–48

8th Sunday
1- Isa 49:14–15
2- 1 Cor 4:1–5
Gospel- Mt 6:24–34

9th Sunday
1- Deut 11:18, 26–28, 32

2- Rom 3:21–25, 28
Gospel- Mt 7:21–27

10th Sunday
1- Hosea 6:3–6
2- Rom 4:18–25
Gospel- Mt 9:9–13

11th Sunday
1- Ex 19:2–6a
2- Rom 5:6–11
Gospel- Mt 9:36—10:8

12th Sunday
1- Jer 20:10–13
2- Rom 5:12–15
Gospel- Mt 10:26–33

13th Sunday
1- 2 Kgs 4:8–11, 14–16a
2- Rom 6:3–4, 8–11
Gospel- Mt 10:37–42

14th Sunday
1- Zech 9:9–10
2- Rom 8:9, 11–13
Gospel- Mt 11:25–30

15th Sunday
1- Isa 55:10–11
2- Rom 8:18–23
Gospel- Mt 13:1–23 or 13:1–9

16th Sunday
1- Wisdom 12:13, 16–19
2- Rom 8:26–27
Gospel- Mt 13:24–43 or 13:24–30

17th Sunday
1- 1 Kgs 3:5, 7–12
2- Rom 8:28–30
Gospel- Mt 13:44–52 or 13:44–46

18th Sunday
1- Isa 55:1–3
2- Rom 8:35, 37–39
Gospel- Mt 14:13–21

19th Sunday
1- 1 Kgs 19:9a, 11–13a
2- Rom 9:1–5
Gospel- Mt 14:22–33

20th Sunday
1- Isa 56:1, 6–7

2- Rom 11:13–15, 29–32
Gospel- Mt 15:21–28

21st Sunday
1- Isa 22:19–23
2- Rom 11:33–36
Gospel- Mt 16:13–20

22nd Sunday
1- Jer 20:7–9
2- Rom 12:1–2
Gospel- Mt 16:21–27

23rd Sunday
1- Ezek 33:7–9
2- Rom 13:8–10
Gospel- Mt 18:15–20

24th Sunday
1- Sirach 27:30—28:9
2- Rom 14:7–9
Gospel- Mt 18:21–35

25th Sunday
1- Isa 55:6–9
2- Phil 1:20c–24, 27a
Gospel- Mt 20:1–16a

26th Sunday
1- Ezek 18:25–28
2- Phil 2:1–11 or 2:1–5
Gospel- Mt 21:28–32

27th Sunday
1- Isa 5:1–7
2- Phil 4:6–9
Gospel- Mt 21:33–43

28th Sunday
1- Isa 25:6–10
2- Phil 4:12–14, 19–20
Gospel- Mt 22:1–14 or 22:1–10

29th Sunday
1- Isa 45:1, 4–6
2- 1 Thes 1:1–5b
Gospel- Mt 22:15–21

30th Sunday
1- Ex 22:20–26
2- 1 Thes 1:5c–10
Gospel- Mt 22:34–40

31st Sunday
1- Mal 1:14b—2:2b, 8–10

2- 1 Thes 2:7b–9, 13
Gospel- Mt 23:1–12

32nd Sunday
1- Wisdom 6:12–16
2- 1 Thes 4:13–18 or 4:13–14
Gospel- Mt 25:1–13

33rd Sunday
1- Prov 31:10–13, 19–20, 30–31
2- 1 Thes 5:1–6
Gospel- Mt 25:14–30 or 25:14–15, 19–21

34th Sunday (Christ the King)
1- Ezek 34:11–12, 15–17
2- 1 Cor 15:20–26, 28
Gospel- Mt 25:31–46

Year B

Cycle of Sunday Readings
2018, 2021, 2024, 2027, 2030

Advent Season

1st Sunday of Advent
1- Isa 63:16b–17, 19b; 64:2–7
2- 1 Cor 1:3–9
Gospel- Mk 13:33–37

2nd Sunday of Advent
1- Isa 40:1–5, 9–11
2- 2 Pt 3:8–14
Gospel- Mk 1:1–8

3rd Sunday of Advent
1- Isa 61:1–2, 10–11
2- 1 Thes 5:16–24
Gospel- Jn 1:6–8, 19–28

4th Sunday of Advent
1- 2 Sam 7:1–5, 8b–12, 14a–16
2- Rom 16:25–27
Gospel- Lk 1:26–38

Christmas Season

Christmas Vigil

1- Isa 62:1–5
2- Acts 13:16–17, 22–25
Gospel- Mt 1:1–25 or 1:18–25

Christmas (at Midnight)
1- Isa 9:1–6
2- Ti 2:11–14
Gospel- Lk 2:1–14

Christmas (at Dawn)
1- Isa 62:11–12
2- Ti 3:4–7
Gospel- Lk 2:15–20

Christmas (during the Day)
1- Isa 52:7–10
2- Heb 1:1–6
Gospel- Jn 1:1–18 or 1:1–5, 9–14

Sunday after Christmas (Holy Family)
1- Gen 15:1–6; 21:1–3
2- Heb 11:8, 11–12, 17–19
Gospel- Lk 2:22–40 or 2:22, 39–40

January 1 (Solemnity of Mary, Mother of God)
1- Num 6:22–27
2- Gal 4:4–7
Gospel- Lk 2:16–21

2nd Sunday after Christmas
1- Sirach 24:1–2, 8–12
2- Eph 1:3–6, 15–18
Gospel- Jn 1:1–18 or 1:1–5, 9–14

Epiphany
1- Isa 60:1–6
2- Eph 3:2–3a, 5–6
Gospel- Mt 2:1–12

Sunday after Epiphany (Baptism of the Lord)
1- Isa 55:1–11
2- 1 Jn 5:1–9
Gospel- Mk 1:7–11

Lenten Season
Ash Wednesday
1- Joel 2:12–18
2- 2 Cor 5:20—6:2
Gospel- Mt 6:1–6, 16–18

1st Sunday of Lent
1- Gen 9:8–15
2- 1 Pt 3:18–22
Gospel- Mk 1:12–15

2nd Sunday of Lent
1- Gen 22:1–2, 9a, 10–13, 15–18

2- Rom 8:31b–34
Gospel- Mk 9:2–10

3rd Sunday of Lent
1- Ex 20:1–17 or 20:1–3, 7–8, 12–17
2- 1 Cor 1:22–25
Gospel- Jn 2:13–25 or 4:5–42

4th Sunday of Lent
1- 2 Chron 36:14–16, 19–23
2- Eph 2:4–10
Gospel- Jn 3:14–21 or 9:1–41

5th Sunday of Lent
1- Jer 31:31–34
2- Heb 5:7–9
Gospel- Jn 12:20–33 or 11:1–45

Passion Sunday (Palm Sunday)
Procession: Mk 11:1–10
or Jn 12:12–16
1- Isa 50:4–7
2- Phil 2:6–11
Gospel- Mk 14:1—15:47 or 15:1–39

Easter Triduum and Easter Season
Holy Thursday, Chrism Mass
1- Isa 61:1–3a, 6ab, 8b–9

2- Rev 1:5–8
Gospel- Lk 4:16–21

Holy Thursday, Mass of the Lord's Supper
1- Ex 12:1–8, 11–14
2- 1 Cor 11:23–26
Gospel- Jn 13:1–15

Good Friday
1- Isa 52:13—53:12
2- Heb 4:14–16; 5:7–9
Gospel- Jn 18:1—19:42

Easter Vigil
1- Gen 1:1—2:2 or 1:1, 26–31a
Gen 22:1–18 or 22:1–2, 9, 10–13, 15–18
Ex 14:15—15:1
Isa 54:5–14
Isa 55:1–11
Baruch 3:9–15, 32—4:4
Ezek 36:16–28
2- Rom 6:3–11
Gospel- Mk 16:1–8

Easter Sunday
1- Acts 10:34a, 37–43
2- Col 3:1–4
or 1 Cor 5:6b–8

Gospel- Jn 20:1–9 or Mk 16:1–8
Evening: Gospel- Lk 24:13–35

2nd Sunday of Easter
1- Acts 4:32–35
2- 1 Jn 5:1–6
Gospel- Jn 20:19–31

3rd Sunday of Easter
1- Acts 3:13–15, 17–19
2- 1 Jn 2:1–5a
Gospel- Lk 24:35–48

4th Sunday of Easter
1- Acts 4:8–12
2- 1 Jn 3:1–2
Gospel- Jn 10:11–18

5th Sunday of Easter
1- Acts 9:26–31
2- 1 Jn 3:18–24
Gospel- Jn 15:1–8

6th Sunday of Easter
1- Acts 10:25–26, 34–35, 44–48
2- 1 Jn 4:7–10
Gospel- Jn 15:9–17

Ascension of Our Lord
1- Acts 1:1–11
2- Eph 1:17–23 or 4:1–13 or 4:1–7, 11–13
Gospel- Mk 16:15–20

7th Sunday of Easter
1- Acts 1:15–17, 20a, 20c–26
2- 1 Jn 4:11–16
Gospel- Jn 17:11b–19

Pentecost Vigil
1- Gen 11:1–9
or Ex 19:3–8a, 16–20b
or Ezek 37:1–14
or Joel 3:1–5
2- Rom 8:22–27
Gospel- Jn 7:37–39

Mass of the Day
1- Acts 2:1–11
2- 1 Cor 12:3b–7, 12–13 or Gal 5:16–25
Gospel- Jn 20:19–23 or 15:26–27; 16:12–15

Solemnities of the Lord during Ordinary Time
Trinity Sunday (Sunday after Pentecost)
1- Deut 4:32–34, 39–40
2- Rom 8:14–17
Gospel- Mt 28:16–20

Corpus Christi
1- Ex 24:3–8
2- Heb 9:11–15
Gospel- Mk 14:12–16, 22–26

Sacred Heart of Jesus (Friday after Corpus Christi)
1- Hosea 11:1, 3–4, 8c–9
2- Eph 3:8–12, 14–19
Gospel- Jn 19:31–37

Ordinary Time
1st Sunday (See Baptism of the Lord, above)
2nd Sunday
1- 1 Sam 3:3b–10, 19
2- 1 Cor 6:13c–15a, 17–20
Gospel- Jn 1:35–42

3rd Sunday
1- Jonah 3:1–5, 10
2- 1 Cor 7:29–31
Gospel- Mk 1:14–20

4th Sunday
1- Deut 18:15–20
2- 1 Cor 7:32–35
Gospel- Mk 1:21–28

5th Sunday
- 1- Job 7:1–4, 6–7
- 2- 1 Cor 9:16–19, 22–23
- Gospel- Mk 1:29–39

6th Sunday
- 1- Lev 13:1–2, 44–46
- 2- 1 Cor 10:31—11:1
- Gospel- Mk 1:40–45

7th Sunday
- 1- Isa 43:18–19, 21–22, 24b–25
- 2- 2 Cor 1:18–22
- Gospel- Mk 2:1–12

8th Sunday
- 1- Hosea 2:16b, 17b, 21–22
- 2- 2 Cor 3:1–6
- Gospel- Mk 2:18–22

9th Sunday
- 1- Deut 5:12–15
- 2- 2 Cor 4:6–11
- Gospel- Mk 2:23—3:6 or 2:23–28

10th Sunday
- 1- Gen 3:9–15

2- 2 Cor 4:13—5:1
Gospel- Mk 3:20–35

11th Sunday
1- Ezek 17:22–24
2- 2 Cor 5:6–10
Gospel- Mk 4:26–34

12th Sunday
1- Job 38:1, 8–11
2- 2 Cor 5:14–17
Gospel- Mk 4:35–41

13th Sunday
1- Wisdom 1:13–15; 2:23–24
2- 2 Cor 8:7, 9, 13–15
Gospel- Mk 5:21–43 or 5:21–24, 35–43

14th Sunday
1- Ezek 2:2–5
2- 2 Cor 12:7–10
Gospel- Mk 6:1–6

15th Sunday
1- Amos 7:12–15
2- Eph 1:3–14 or 1:3–10
Gospel- Mk 6:7–13

16th Sunday
1- Jer 23:1–6
2- Eph 2:13–18
Gospel- Mk 6:30–34

17th Sunday
1- 2 Kgs 4:42–44
2- Eph 4:1–6
Gospel- Jn 6:1–15

18th Sunday
1- Ex 16:2–4, 12–15
2- Eph 4:17, 20–24
Gospel- Jn 6:24–35

19th Sunday
1- 1 Kgs 19:4–8
2- Eph 4:30—5:2
Gospel- Jn 6:41–51

20th Sunday
1- Prov 9:1–6
2- Eph 5:15–20
Gospel- Jn 6:51–58

21st Sunday
1- Josh 24:1–2a, 15–17, 18b

2- Eph 5:21–32 or 5:2a, 25–32
Gospel- Jn 6:60–69

22nd Sunday
1- Deut 4:1–2, 6–8
2- Jms 1:17–18, 21b–22, 27
Gospel- Mk 7:1–8, 14–15, 21–23

23rd Sunday
1- Isa 35:4–7a
2- Jms 2:1–5
Gospel- Mk 7:31–37

24th Sunday
1- Isa 50:5–9a
2- Jms 2:14–18
Gospel- Mk 8:27–35

25th Sunday
1- Wisdom 2:12, 17–20
2- Jms 3:16—4:3
Gospel- Mk 9:30–37

26th Sunday
1- Num 11:25–29
2- Jms 5:1–6
Gospel- Mk 9:38–43, 45, 47–48

27th Sunday
1- Gen 2:18–24
2- Heb 2:9–11
Gospel- Mk 10:2–16 or 10:2–12

28th Sunday
1- Wisdom 7:7–11
2- Heb 4:12–13
Gospel- Mk 10:17–30 or 10:17–27

29th Sunday
1- Isa 53:10–11
2- Heb 4:14–16
Gospel- Mk 10:35–45 or 10:42–45

30th Sunday
1- Jer 31:7–9
2- Heb 5:1–6
Gospel- Mk 10:46–52

31st Sunday
1- Deut 6:2–6
2- Heb 7:23–28
Gospel- Mk 12:28–34

32nd Sunday
1- 1 Kgs 17:10–16

2- Heb 9:24–28
Gospel- Mk 12:38–44 or 12:41–44

33rd Sunday
1- Dan 12:1–3
2- Heb 10:11–14, 18
Gospel- Mk 13:24–32

34th Sunday (Christ the King)
1- Dan 7:13–14
2- Rev 1:5–8
Gospel- Jn 18:33b–37

Year C

Cycle of Sunday readings
2019, 2022, 2025, 2028, 2031

Advent Season

1st Sunday of Advent
1- Jer 33:14–16
2- 1 Thes 3:12—4:2
Gospel- Lk 21:25–28, 34–36

2nd Sunday of Advent
1- Baruch 5:1–9
2- Phil 1:4–6, 8–11
Gospel- Lk 3:1–6

3rd Sunday of Advent
1- Zeph 3:14–18a
2- Phil 4:4–7
Gospel- Lk 3:10–18

4th Sunday of Advent
1- Micah 5:1–4a
2- Heb 10:5–10
Gospel- Lk 1:39–45

Christmas Season

Christmas Vigil

1- Isa 62:1–6
2- Acts 13:16–17, 22–25
Gospel- Mt 1:1–25 or 1:18–25

Christmas (at Midnight)
1- Isa 9:1–6
2- Ti 2:11–14
Gospel- Lk 2:1–14

Christmas (at Dawn)
1- Isa 62:11–12
2- Ti 3:4–7
Gospel- Lk 2:15–20

Christmas (during the Day)
1- Isa 57:7–10
2- Heb 1:1–6
Gospel- Jn 1:1–18 or 1:1–5, 9–14

Sunday after Christmas (Holy Family)
1- 1 Sam 1:20–22, 24–28
2- 1 Jn 3:1–2, 21–24
Gospel- Lk 2:41–52

January 1 (Solemnity of Mary, Mother of God)
1- Num 6:22–27
2- Gal 4:4–7
Gospel- Lk 2:16–21

2nd Sunday After Christmas
1- Sirach 24:1–2, 8–12
2- Eph 1:3–6, 15–18
Gospel- Jn 1:1–18 or 1:1–5, 9–14

Epiphany
1- Isa 60:1–6
2- Eph 3:2–3a, 5–6
Gospel- Mt 2:1–12

Sunday after Epiphany (Baptism of the Lord)
1- Isa 40:1–5, 9–11
2- Titus 2:11–14; 3:4–7
Gospel- Lk 3:15–16, 21–22

Lenten Season
Ash Wednesday
1- Joel 2:12–18
2- 2 Cor 5:20—6:2
Gospel- Mt 6:1–6, 16–18

1st Sunday of Lent
1- Deut 26:4–10
2- Rom 10:8–13
Gospel- Lk 4:1–13

2nd Sunday of Lent
1- Gen 15:5–12, 17–18

2- Phil 3:17—4:1 or 3:20—4:1
Gospel- Lk 9:28b–36

3rd Sunday of Lent
1- Ex 3:1–8a, 13–15
2- 1 Cor 10:1–6, 10–12
Gospel- Lk 13:1–9 or Jn 4:5–42

4th Sunday of Lent
1- Josh 5:9a, 10–12
2- 2 Cor 5:17–21
Gospel- Lk 15:1–3, 11–32 or Jn 9:1–41

5th Sunday of Lent
1- Isa 43:16–21
2- Phil 3:8–14
Gospel- Jn 8:1–11 or 11:1–45

Passion Sunday (Palm Sunday)
Procession: Lk 19:28–40
1- Isa 50:4–7
2- Phil 2:6–11
Gospel- Lk 22:14—23:56 or 23:1–49

Easter Triduum and Easter Season
Holy Thursday, Chrism Mass
1- Isa 61:1–3ab, 6a, 8b–9

2- Rev 1:5–8
Gospel- Lk 4:16–21

Holy Thursday, Mass of the Lord's Supper
1- Ex 12:1–8, 11–14
2- 1 Cor 11:23–26
Gospel- Jn 13:1–15

Good Friday
1- Isa 52:13—53:12
2- Heb 4:14–16; 5:7–9
Gospel- Jn 18:1—19:42

Easter Vigil
1- Gen 1:1—2:2 or 1:1, 26–31a
Gen 22:1–18 or 22:1–2, 9, 10–13, 15–18
Ex 14:15—15:1
Isa 54:5–14
Isa 55:1–11
Baruch 3:9–15, 32—4:4
Ezek 36:16–28
2- Rom 6:3–11
Gospel- Lk 24:1–12

Easter Sunday
1- Acts 10:34a, 37–43
2- Col 3:1–4 or 1 Cor 5:6b–8

Gospel- Jn 20:1–9 or Lk 24:1–12
Evening: Gospel- Lk 24:13–35

2nd Sunday of Easter
1- Acts 5:12–16
2- Rev 1:9–11a, 12–13, 17–19
Gospel- Jn 20:19–31

3rd Sunday of Easter
1- Acts 5:27b–32, 40b–41
2- Rev 5:11–14
Gospel- Jn 2l:1–19 or 21:1–14

4th Sunday of Easter
1- Acts 13:14, 43–52
2- Rev 7:9, 14b–17
Gospel- Jn 10:27–30

5th Sunday of Easter
1- Acts 14:21–27
2- Rev 21:1–5a
Gospel- Jn 13:31–33a, 34–35

6th Sunday of Easter
1- Acts 15:1–2, 22–29
2- Rev 21:10–14, 22–23
Gospel- Jn 14:23–29

Ascension of the Lord
1- Acts 1:1–11
2- Eph 1:17–23 or Heb 9:24–28; 10:19–23
Gospel- Lk 24:46–53

7th Sunday of Easter
1- Acts 7:55–60
2- Rev 22:12–14, 16–17, 20
Gospel- Jn 17:20–26

Pentecost Vigil
1- Gen 11:1–9 or Ex 19:3–8a, 16–20b
or Ezek 37:1–14 or Joel 3:1–5
2- Rom 8:22–27
Gospel- Jn 7:37–39

Mass of the Day
1- Acts 2:1–11
2- 1 Cor 12:3b–7, 12–13 or Rom 8:8–17
Gospel- Jn 20:19–23 or Jn 14:15–16, 23b–26

Solemnities of the Lord During Ordinary

Trinity Sunday (Sunday after Pentecost)
1- Prov 8:22–31
2- Rom 5:1–5
Gospel- Jn 16:12–15

Corpus Christi
1- Gen 14:18–20
2- 1 Cor 11:23–26
Gospel- Lk 9:11b–17

Sacred Heart of Jesus (Friday after Corpus Christi)
1- Ezek 34:11–16
2- Rom 5:5b–11
Gospel- Lk 15:3–7

Ordinary Time
1st Sunday (See Baptism of the Lord, above)
2nd Sunday
1- Isa 62:1–5
2- 1 Cor 12:4–11
Gospel- Jn 2:1–11

3rd Sunday
1- Neh 8:2–4a, 5–6, 8–10
2- 1 Cor 12:12–30 or 12:12–14, 27
Gospel- Lk 1:1–4; 4:14–21

4th Sunday
1- Jer 1:4–5, 17–19
2- 1 Cor 12:31—13:13 or 13:4–13
Gospel- Lk 4:21–30

5th Sunday
1- Isa 6:1–2a, 3–8
2- 1 Cor 15:1–11 or 15:3–8, 11
Gospel- Lk 5:1–11

6th Sunday
1- Jer 17:5–8
2- 1 Cor 15:12, 16–20
Gospel- Lk 6:17, 20–26

7th Sunday
1- 1 Sam 26:2, 7–9, 12–13, 22–23
2- 1 Cor 15:45–49
Gospel- Lk 6:27–38

8th Sunday
1- Sirach 27:4–7
2- 1 Cor 15:54–58
Gospel- Lk 6:39–45

9th Sunday
1- 1 Kgs 8:41–43
2- Gal 1:1–2, 6–10
Gospel- Lk 7:1–10

10th Sunday
1- 1 Kgs 17:17–24

2- Gal 1:11–19
Gospel- Lk 7:11–17

11th Sunday
1- 2 Sam 12:7–10, 13
2- Gal 2:16, 19–21
Gospel- Lk 7:36—8:3 or 7:36–50

12th Sunday
1- Zech 12:10–11; 13:1
2- Gal 3:26–29
Gospel- Lk 9:18–24

13th Sunday
1- 1 Kgs 19:16b, 19–21
2- Gal 5:1, 13–18
Gospel- Lk 9:51–62

14th Sunday
1- Isa 66:10–14c
2- Gal 6:14–18
Gospel- Lk 10:1–12, 17–20 or 10:1–9

15th Sunday
1- Deut 30:10–14
2- Col 1:15–20
Gospel- Lk 10:25–37

16th Sunday
1- Gen 18:1–10a
2- Col 1:24–28
Gospel- Lk 10:38–42

17th Sunday
1- Gen 18:20–32
2- Col 2:12–14
Gospel- Lk 11:1–13

18th Sunday
1- Eccl 1:2; 2:21–23
2- Col 3:1–5, 9–11
Gospel- Lk 12:13–21

19th Sunday
1- Wisdom 18:6–9
2- Heb 11:1–2, 8–19 or 11:1–2, 8–12
Gospel- Lk 12:32–48 or 12:35–40

20th Sunday
1- Jer 38:4–6, 8–10
2- Heb 12:1–4
Gospel- Lk 12:49–53

21st Sunday
1- Isa 66:18–21

2- Heb 12:5–7, 11–13
Gospel- Lk 13:22–30

22nd Sunday
1- Sirach 3:17–18, 20, 28–29
2- Heb 12:18–19, 22–24a
Gospel- Lk 14:1, 7–14

23rd Sunday
1- Wisdom 9:13–18b
2- Phlm 9–10, 12–17
Gospel- Lk 14:25–33

24th Sunday
1- Ex 32:7–11, 13–14
2- 1 Tm 1:12–17
Gospel- Lk 15:1–32 or 15:1–10

25th Sunday
1- Amos 8:4–7
2- 1 Tm 2:1–8
Gospel- Lk 16:1–13 or 16:10–13

26th Sunday
1- Amos 6:1, 4–7
2- 1 Tm 6:11–16
Gospel- Lk 16:19–31

27th Sunday
1- Hab 1:2–3; 2:2–4
2- 2 Tm 1:6–8, 13–14
Gospel- Lk 17:5–10

28th Sunday
1- 2 Kgs 5:14–17
2- 2 Tm 2:8–13
Gospel- Lk 17:11–19

29th Sunday
1- Ex 17:8–13
2- 2 Tm 3:14—4:2
Gospel- Lk 18:1–8

30th Sunday
1- Sirach 35:12–14, 16–18
2- 2 Tm 4:6–8, 16–18
Gospel- Lk 18:9–14

31st Sunday
1- Wisdom 11:22—12:2
2- 2 Thes 1:11—2:2
Gospel- Lk 19:1–10

32nd Sunday
1- 2 Macc 7:1–2, 9–14

2- 2 Thes 2:16—3:5
Gospel- Lk 20:27–38 or 20:27, 34–38

33rd Sunday
1- Mal 3:19–20
2- 2 Thes 3:7–12
Gospel- Lk 21:5–19

34th Sunday (Christ the King)
1- 2 Sam 5:1–3
2- Col 1:12–20
Gospel- Lk 23:35–43

APPENDIX 2

Suggested Reading List: Other Biblical Resources to Help You Go Deeper

An Overview of Biblical Books

You Can Understand the Bible: A Practical and Illuminating Guide to Each Book of the Bible, Peter Kreeft

The Quick Reference Guide to the Catholic Bible, Mary Ann Getty Sullivan

New Testament Basics for Catholics, John Bergsma

A Catholic Introduction to the Bible: The Old Testament, Brant Pitre and John Bergsma

Biblical Commentaries

The Catholic Study Bible (New American Bible Revised Edition, published by Oxford University Press) and *The New Jerusalem Bible* (published by Doubleday) have good reading guides and notes.

The New Jerome Biblical Commentary, Raymond E. Brown, SS, editor

The Collegeville Bible Commentary, Robert J. Karris, editor

The Catholic Commentary on Sacred Scripture series, Peter Williamson and Mary Healy, editors

An Overview of Salvation History

Bible Basics for Catholics: A New Picture of Salvation History, John Bergsma

A Father Who Keeps His Promises, Scott Hahn

Walking with God: A Journey through the Bible, Jeff Cavins and Tim Gray

Jesus the Bridegroom: The Greatest Love Story Ever Told, Brant Pitre

Scripture and Prayer

Christian Prayer (for praying the Liturgy of the Hours)

Conversing with God in Scripture: A Contemporary Approach to Lectio Divina, Stephen J. Binz

Catholic Bible Study Series

The Keys to the Bible Series (The Word Among Us Press)
Little Rock Scripture Study (Diocese of Little Rock and Liturgical Press)

Six Weeks with the Bible (Loyola Press)
Threshold Bible Study (Twenty-Third Publications)

And if you enjoyed *Unleashing the Power of Scripture*, **here are some other titles and resources by Mark Hart:**

Books

A Second Look: Encountering the True Jesus
Ascend: A Companion to the Sunday Mass Readings
Ask the Bible Geek: Fascinating Answers to Intriguing Questions
Ask the Bible Geek 2: More Answers to Questions from Catholic Teens
Behold the Mystery: A Deeper Understanding of theCatholic Mass
Blessed Are the Bored in Spirit: A Young Catholic's Search for Meaning
Embracing God's Plan for Marriage: A Scripture Study for Couples
Holier than Thou: Amazing Saint Stories You Have to Read to Believe
The "R" Father: 14 Ways to Respond to the Lord's Prayer
Tweet Inspiration: Faith in 140 Characters or Less

Zealous: Following Jesus with Guidance from Saint Paul
100 Things Every Catholic Teen Should Know

Video Bible Study Series

For High Schoolers and Young Adults:
T3 The Teen Timeline
T3 Matthew: Thy Kingdom Come
T3 Acts: The Keys and the Sword
T3 Revelation: The Lion and the Lamb

For Middle Schoolers:
Encounter: Experiencing God in the Every Day

For All Ages:
Altaration: The Mystery of the Mass Revealed

Notes

1. Pope Francis, homily remarks, April 24, 2013 (Vatican City: Catholic News Agency), http://www.catholicnewsagency.com/news/church-is-a-love-story-pope-francis-says/.

2. Pope Pius XII, *Divino Afflante Spiritu* [Inspired by the Holy Spirit], September 30, 1943, 35–36.

3. Pope St. John Paul II, Letter to Families, February 22, 1994, 11.

4. Mark Giszczak, *Light on the Dark Passages of Scripture* (Huntington, IN: Our Sunday Visitor, 2015), 41.
5. Giszczak, 178.

6. See my book *A Second Look: Encountering the True Jesus* (Huntington, IN: Our Sunday Visitor, 2016).

7. St Augustine, *Against the Letter of Mani Called "The Foundation,"* 5:6

8. G.K. Chesterton, *Orthodoxy* (New York: SnowBall Classics, 2015), p. 78.

9. See my book *Behold the Mystery: A Better Understanding of the Catholic Mass* (Ijamsville, MD: The Word Among Us, 2014).

10. See my book *The "R" Father: 14 Ways to Respond to the Lord's Prayer* (Ijamsville, MD: The Word Among Us, 2010).

11. See *Behold the Mystery*.

12. See *A Second Look*.

This book was published by The Word Among Us. Since 1981, The Word Among Us has been answering the call of the Second Vatican Council to help Catholic laypeople encounter Christ in the Scriptures.

The name of our company comes from the prologue to the Gospel of John and reflects the vision and purpose of all of our publications: to be an instrument of the Spirit, whose desire is to manifest Jesus' presence in and to the children of God. In this way, we hope to contribute to the Church's ongoing mission of proclaiming the gospel to the world so that all people would know the love and mercy of our Lord and grow more deeply in their faith as missionary disciples.

Our monthly devotional magazine, *The Word Among Us*, features meditations on the daily and Sunday Mass readings, and currently reaches more than one million Catholics in North America and another half million Catholics in one hundred countries around the world. Our book division, The Word Among Us Press, publishes numerous books, Bible studies, and pamphlets that help Catholics grow in their faith.

To learn more about who we are and what we publish, log on to our website at www.wau.org. There you will find a variety of Catholic resources that will help you grow in your faith.

Embrace His Word, Listen to God . . .

www.wau.org